C000006739

To

Betty
Brownie friendly

BRUM
UNDAUNTED

BIRMINGHAM DURING THE BLITZ

'Smilin' through!': air raid damage in Wood End
Road, Erdington, 16 August 1940.
Courtesy of Birmingham Post and Mail Ltd.

Carl Chinn

remembering the old end

best wishes

Carl Chinn

To all those Brummies who collared and fought for freedom.
We shall not forget.

Copyright © 1996 Carl Chinn

The right of Carl Chinn to be identified as the author of this work has been asserted by him in accordance with the Copyright, Designs and Patents Act 1988.

This book is sold subject to the condition that it shall not, by way of trade or otherwise, be lent, re-sold, hired out or otherwise circulated without the publisher's prior consent in any form of binding or cover other than that in which it is published and without a similar condition being imposed on the subsequent purchaser.

No part of this publication may be reproduced or transmitted, in any form or by any means, electronic or mechanical, including photocopying, recording or any information storage or retrieval system, without either the prior permission in writing from the publisher or a licence, permitting restricted copying. In the United Kingdom such licences are issued by the Copyright Licensing Agency, 90 Tottenham Court Road, London W1P 9HE.

CIP catalogue record for this book is available from the British Library.

ISBN 0 7093 0218 5

Photograph credits
All photographs and illustrations are courtesy of the Birmingham Post and Mail Ltd, except for those from the Hulton Getty Collection, pp. 12, 13, 14, 15, 17; John Essex, pp. 49 and 64; Stella Couper, p. 7; Winnie Martin, p. 9; Birmingham Library Services, p. 28; John Shepherd, p. 31; Cliff Casson, p. 36; Sheila Swan, p. 41; John Marks, p. 60; Michael and Vera Mattiello, p. 66; Ivy Jackson, p. 113; June Eastlake, p. 128; Jean Allen, p. 131; and Kitty Bell, p. 137.

Published by Birmingham Library Services

Designed and produced by Citypack Ltd 0121 622 3384

CONTENTS

TIME CHART

1933	Hitler comes to power in Germany.
1936 *to 1938*	The Great Terror of Stalin in the Soviet Union.
1937 *April 26*	German bombing of Basque town of Guernica in Spanish Civil War.
1938 *March 12*	The *Anschluss*, take-over of Austria by Germany.
1938 *September 29*	Neville Chamberlain, Prime Minister of the United Kingdom and Edouard Daladier, Prime Minister of France, agree to Germans taking over the Sudetenland from Czechoslovakia.
1938 *October*	German annexation of the Sudetenland from Czechoslovakia.

1939

March	Victory of Franco and the defeat of the Republicans in the Spanish Civil War.
May 22	Pact of Steel between Germany and Italy.
August 23	Non-Aggression Pact between Hitler and Stalin.
August 25	Anglo-Polish Alliance.
September 1	German invasion of Poland.
	Air Raid Precautions and overall running of Birmingham to be supervised by Emergency Committee.
	Official Evacuation begins in Birmingham and other British cities.
September 3	United Kingdom and France declare war on Germany.
September 27	Poland defeated.
November 15	Delivery of 100,000th Anderson Shelter to Birmingham.

1940

April 9	German troops occupy Denmark and invade Norway.
May 10	Germany attacks Netherlands and Belgium.
	Resignation of Neville Chamberlain as Prime Minister of United Kingdom; replaced by Winston Churchill.
May 14	German bombing of Rotterdam; over 900 people killed.
	Germans break through French defences.
	Formation of Home Guard.
May 28	Surrender of Belgium.
May 26 to June 4	British Expeditionary Force evacuated from Dunkirk.
June 21	France signs armistice with victorious Germans.
July	Battle of Britain begins.
August 9	First air raid on Birmingham; bombs dropped on Erdington.
August 25	Major night raid on Birmingham City Centre; the Market Hall burned out.
September 15	RAF victorious in Battle of Britain.
October 24	Shelter hit in Cox Street, Hockley; 25 people killed.
October 25	Nineteen people die when a bomb lands on the 'Carlton' Picture House, Sparkbrook.
October 26	Explosives blast first-aid post at Kent Street Baths; many casualties. Fifteen people killed in a shelter in Barker Street, Summer Hill.

November 14	Fierce raid on Coventry, described as 'Our Guernica'.
November 15	Death of Neville Chamberlain.
November 19	Heavy raids across central Birmingham. BSA, Small Heath hit and 53 workers killed. Grant Street, off Holloway Head devastated by a land mine. Great damage in Hockley, Snow Hill, Lozells, Saltley and many other neighbourhoods. An estimated 615 Brummies killed.
November 20	Queens Road, Aston almost obliterated by a naval mine.
November 22	Further heavy raids on Birmingham, especially on the east and centre of the city.
December 11	Another heavy raid on Birmingham; St Thomas's, Bath Row virtually destroyed.
December 12	King George VI visits blitzed neighbourhoods in Birmingham.

1941

April 9	Major attack on Birmingham. Widespread damage; The Prince of Wales Theatre, Broad Street destroyed.
June 22	Germany attacks USSR.
December 7	Japanese attack U.S. Navy at Pearl Harbor and invade Malaya and the Philippines.

1942

June 3	U.S. win Battle of Midway and stop Japanese expansion in the Pacific.
July 27	Bombs cause deaths and damage in Birmingham, especially in Rookery Road, Handsworth.
July 30	Last main air raid on Birmingham.
November 4	British victory at El Alamein, North Africa.

1943

April 23	Final German attack on Birmingham by a lone raider bombing Drummond Road, Little Bromwich.
July 25	Fall of Mussolini in Italy.
September 3	Italy surrenders to the Allies.

1944

January	Massive Soviet offensive against the Germans in the east.
June 6	D-Day landings by Allies in Normandy.

1945

April 30	Hitler commits suicide.
May 2	Berlin falls to the Red Army.
May 8	Victory in Europe Day.
August 15	Victory against Japan Day.

ACKNOWLEDGEMENTS

I have been fortunate that many people have helped me with my research for this book. Numerous Brummies have written me letters about their experiences of life during the Second World War and have provided me with an evocative first-hand source. I am grateful to them for their generosity and kindness and have acknowledged them when I have used such a recollection. These personal memories have been enhanced by stunning photographs taken during the war. Most of them have never been published before. They are from the archives of the Birmingham Evening Mail and I thank Ian Dowell, Editor, and John Daniels, Managing Editor of the Birmingham Post, Evening Mail and Sunday Mercury for allowing me to use them. Similarly, I am grateful to Birmingham Library Services for access to the city's magnificent archives and local studies collection, and for the publication of this book. I thank Hulton Getty Collection for permission to reproduce five photographs in the Introduction. I thank also a number of friends and colleagues who have given me support and assistance: Martin Flynn, Central Library Manager at Birmingham Central Library, who has co-ordinated the business side of this work; Richard Albutt, Community History Development Librarian at Birmingham Central Library, who scanned masses of material for me; Graham Bragg, Photographic Technician at the Birmingham Evening Mail, who reproduced photographs from glass negatives dating from the war; Mike Evetts, a librarian at the Birmingham Evening Mail, who alerted me to the existence of three volumes of newspaper cuttings on our city during the war; Mr A.R. Vincent Daviss, formerly of Gillott Lodge, Gillott Road who compiled those cuttings and which have been an invaluable source; Bill McCarthy, Special Publications, Birmingham Evening Mail, and Pam Wilkinson, Co-ordinator Birmingham Voice, for passing on to me letters about the war; Graham Caldicott, Ian Hinton and Gary Hassle - all of the Birmingham Evening Mail - for their backing; Dr John Bourne, for his constructive criticism; and Alan Mahar, Sally Moore, Jim Warren and everyone at Citypack, where this book was designed. Collectively, I appreciate the helpfulness of all the librarians at the Evening Mail, of numerous librarians from Birmingham Library Services and all the folk who have contributed memories by way of my show on BBC Radio WM. In particular, I pay tribute to the determination and dedication of Marjorie Ashby who has striven to make known the facts about the Blitz on Birmingham and who has campaigned tirelessly for a memorial to its victims. Most of all I thank my family for their continued backing, and especially I say 'ta' to my wife Kay for her understanding and patience.

FOREWORD

I was born eleven years after V.E. Day. Like all of my generation I may not have lived through the Second World War but we lived with it. Every Sunday dinner-time we knew we had to sit up and take notice when Our Dad said, 'In the war'. Usually he went on, 'See that bit of meat on your plates, you've got that for one dinner. That was our meat ration for a week. You don't know how lucky you are.' And if ever we said we were full-up and couldn't eat anything else then we were set for a proper lecture. 'D'you know', the Old Man'd go, 'in the war the poor Poles'd've given anything to have what you're leaving on the plate. You ought to be ashamed of yourselves, wasting good food. The Poles had nothing, they starved. So eat up.' It was a regular thing for us to hear not only about the hardships of the Poles but also of their valour. We listened with awe about how their cavalry charged against the tanks of the Germans even though they knew they were doomed to failure and probably would be killed. And with horror we learned of how Polish Jews courageously fought the better-armed and more numerous Nazis and were finally pushed back to a last-desperate resistance in the sewers of Warsaw.

Much of what we were told we could watch on *All Our Yesterdays*, a television programme which described what happened to the world day-by-day between 1939 and 45. But it wasn't just on the TV that we saw the war. It was all around us in Birmingham - in numerous large and small bomb pecks which bore witness to the ferocity of the air raids which had laid waste so much of our city, and in the many terraces of older houses which were broken up by new buildings erected on a site blasted by German bombers. Whenever we passed such places Our Mom and Dad would tell me and Our Kid, Darryl, about their experiences of the war. Our Mom has vague recollections of her evacuation with Our Nan to Cheltenham, whilst the Old Man went with Clifton Road School to Coalville in Leicestershire. Along with so many kids, they returned to Brum during the phoney war and went through the bombing of 1940 and 1941.

Above all, it's the Blitz which has imprinted itself deeply on their memories. They remember many frightening occasions. Like when a high explosive bomb hit Great-Granny

My Great-Granny Chinn and Aunt Betty outside 54, Alfred Street, Sparkbrook, destroyed by bombing in the war.

Chinn's at 54, Alfred Street, Sparkbrook and Billy the Fire Watcher from Gorton's Woodyard came chasing down to Our Grandad's at number 19, popped his head round the door and shouted: 'Alf! Alf! Brockton's house has been hit'. With great-uncle Wal they ran down the road and found that the back of the building had been blown away. Digging furiously through the rubble they found Great-Granny Chinn alive, hidden beneath a sheet of corrugated iron which Our Grandad had put under her stairs to protect her. Then there were the times that land mines obliterated Alfred Road, when the Lansdown Laundry in Studley Street was turned into an inferno, and when Ten House Row in Queen Street was destroyed. We were struck by the acts of bravery which abounded when the bombs came pelting down. There was the gallant Joey Jones, on leave from the Royal Navy, who saw an incendiary device land upstairs in Mr Frost's house. Straight away Joey shot inside, picked up the boiling-hot bomb and threw it through the window. So badly was he burned that he needed skin grafts. And there was the tragedy on the Stratford Road, not far from the Piccadilly picture house, when an explosive fell but didn't detonate. Sandbags and barriers were put round the scene, to keep people back whilst the bomb disposal men went to work. The sergeant had just given his officer some tools and was walking away when the UXB blew up, hurtling him back about twenty yards and killing the valiant officer.

Our Mom and Dad never hid the horror of war, nor did they pretend they hadn't been scared. They drew a vivid picture of deep-black nights when the skies were lit up by scouring searchlights, the fleeting trace of ack-ack guns and an awful multitude of blazes. They evoked the wail of the sirens, the distressing hum of enemy planes and the heart-stopping thud of the bombs as they hit their targets. They summoned up the whiff of gas escaping from blasted pipes, the reek of smoke from burning buildings, and the damp odour arising from water-sodden ground. Through them we touched shrapnel, tasted dried eggs and got the colly-wobbles as the barrage began. Our Mom remembers especially one night of fear when Our Nan and Grandad Perry grabbed her in her night-clothes, held her in their arms and with everyone else rushed down the middle of Whitehouse Street to the big underground shelter of Powell and Hamner's. On another occasion they were in the shelter in their yard and looking through its doorway Our Mom started to blart because it appeared that all the houses in their terrace were alight. They weren't - it was the reflection from the fire which was raging nearby at Rippingilles, the stove manufacturer on the Aston Road North - but to a young child it seemed that her whole world had become a dreadful bonfire. Our Dad also had scares. He and his seven brothers and sisters slept sheltered in their cellar while Our Grandad was out on A.R.P. duty. Once Our Uncle Ron woke up in the pitch dark, thinking a raid was on and that they were trapped. He roared 'Come on, we can get out! This way!' and crawled over the coal and up through the grille to the entry, while Our Dad and the others were shouting in fright. Luckily, the bombing had finished that night and Our Grandad came downstairs and calmed them.

As we listened to these tales we found it hard to believe that there could be any happiness or fun during such terrible times. Yet there was. Our Aunt Win still titters about sending Our Mom to get her sand from the bomb sites so that she could wet it and rub it on her legs. Then she'd get a black pencil and put a line down the back of each of her calves. That way when she went dancing she looked like she had stockings on - except that when she jitterbugged the chaps'd throw her around, her frock'd go up and you could see the whites of her legs above her knees. At one dance Our Win met an American soldier and he came calling for her the next day. Our Great-Grandad Wood answered the door and the GI said, 'Hi, is·blue eyes in'. The reply was swift, short and sharp, 'I'll give you bleedin blue eyes!' and the big American fled down the street pursued by little Grandad Wood. Being younger, Our Mom's memory of the GIs is of trailing behind them as they marched along and calling out with the other kids, 'Got any gum, chum!'

We realised from an early age that you could have a laugh in the midst of troubles, and we were also aware of the power of singing in getting people through bad times. In Our Mom's yard only Mrs Coverson had an Anderson Shelter, hidden beneath grass, dirt and sandbags. Sometimes our lot would go in there and the two families'd have a good sing-along to keep up their spirits. There's one song in particular from those days that has great meaning for all of us, even now. When Our Nan married she got a house in the same street as her Mom and having a

A war-time wedding, 4 August 1945, St Mary's Church, Aston Road North. Most of the adults are servicemen or war workers. Back: John Jennings, Royal Artillery; Nancy Cotterill, husband in RAF ground crew; Arthur Perry, reserved occupation, Die Castings, Highgate; Lil Perry, Powell and Hamner's, Chester Street; Georgie Wood, 2nd Battalion SAS. Middle: Freddie Hodson, Tubes Ltd, Rocky Lane; Bert Martin of South Shields, Petty Officer Stoker, Royal Navy; Winnie Wood, Midland Wheel, Avenue Road; Billy Wood, stoker Royal Navy; Nancy Wood. Front: Gladys Jennings, BSA, Small Heath; Joannie Haddock; Rene Carter, Midland Wheel; May Hodson, G. W. Pearce, Chester Street.

spare bedroom she took in her brother, Our Alfie, and her sister, Our Winnie. When Our Mom came along in 1936 these two meant everything to her and she swore she'd marry Our Alfie. Then as a seventeen-year old he joined the Royal Navy and was sent away. Just four years of age Our Mom couldn't cope. She wouldn't eat and she was pining badly. They wrote to the Navy and Our Alfie was sent back on compassionate leave. As he got off the tram before Aston Cross, one of his mates dragged him into 'The Albion' for a quick pint. Before he could knock it back, word went round Whitehouse Street that he was home. Someone ran down the entry, up the yard and into Our Nan's house, blurting out the news. Our Mom made a swift recovery and raced to the pub. The blokes put her on the bar and with her eyes only on Our Alfie she sang Alice Faye's hit, 'You'll never know just how much I love you'.

My generation never went through the terror of the Second World War, nor did we experience the camaraderie and companionship which were ever-present. We can never know what it was like. But we do know the debt we owe to all of you who collared and fought for freedom. We know that without you we might not be here. We know that without you the United Kingdom might have been subjected to tyranny and brutality. It is a debt we can pay back in only one way. We shall not forget. When you are gone you shall live on. We shall recount with pride your deeds of heroism and your defiance of evil. With swelling hearts we shall tell our children and our children's children of how you stood tall and did not bow before oppression and vileness. Generations yet unborn shall know that you gave us life and liberty. We shall remember.

INTRODUCTION
THE PATH TO WAR

Birmingham was renowned for the variety of its trades and for the skills and adaptibility of its workers. These factors allowed the city's manufacturers to shift swiftly from peace-time production to war work. The results were spectacular. Between 1939 and 1945 Brummies made a wide range of wares which were vital to the British forces and to the defeat of the Germans. Indeed the ouput from Birmingham's factories was greater than that of any other place except for London - and the capital had a population nine times greater than that of Brum. Hitler and his strategists knew that if the Germans were to be victorious then the *Luftwaffe* had to achieve two objectives: to destroy or hamper the British munitions industries; and to cut off supplies of weaponry and food from the United States of America. For these reasons the *Führer* ordered the bombing of British ports and industrial centres.

Birmingham itself was bombed between 9 August 1940 and 23 April 1943, although the main German attacks on the city lasted for nine months until April 1941. In total, Brummies endured 65 air raids during which 2,241 people were killed. But Birmingham was not the only British city which suffered severe bombing. London was hit the hardest of all by the *Luftwaffe* during the Blitz of 1940/41; and in 1944/45 it took the main brunt of the attacks by flying bombs and long-range rockets - although many fell in Kent and Sussex. The German air force also made heavy raids on other places which were crucial to war work such as Coventry, Leicester, Manchester, Nottingham, Sheffield and Sunderland; whilst its bombers caused many deaths and great damage in a number of ports, including Belfast, Bristol, Cardiff, Dover, Glasgow, Great Yarmouth, Hull, Liverpool, Newcastle, Plymouth, Portsmouth and Swansea. Air raids killed folk in many other towns and cities - from South Shields to Canterbury and from Norwich to Exeter. These British people died for the same reason as did millions of others in Europe, Asia and Africa: they died because some leaders were consumed by intolerance, hatred and prejudice; they died because some nations were determined to dominate others; and they died because diplomacy and talking gave way to war and fighting.

Tensions had been growing in Europe throughout the 1930s. In the Soviet Union, Joseph Stalin had eliminated his rivals in the Communist Party and had become an unchallenged dictator. Through posters, slogans and other forms of propaganda he projected a cult of the leader. He was not on his own. In Italy, the fascist Benito Mussolini ruled without an opposition or free press, intimidating communists, socialists, trade unionists, peasants and anyone else who disagreed with him. Dressed in a black, militaristic uniform he adopted the title of *Il Duce*, and wherever he went he was accompanied by militiamen who greeted him with arms outstretched and who accorded him the status of a Roman Emperor. Mussolini was not satisfied with his powerful position within his own country. He sought to gain an empire for Italy, sending forces to conquer Libya, Somalia and Abyssinia. Italian victories were accompanied by indiscriminate air attacks, the use of poison gas and the carrrying out of atrocities.

Within Italy, Mussolini's control was checked partially by the independence of the army, the Catholic Church and the monarchy. There were no such restraints on Adolf Hitler in Germany. During the 1920s he had turned the extremist Nazi Party into a strong organisation with a large membership focused on himself as the dominant figure. Racist, anti-Semitic and excessively nationalistic, bands of Nazis assaulted political rivals and struck fear into those who opposed them. As the world Depression plunged nations into debt and mass unemployment, Hitler and his followers blamed Jews, Bolsheviks and capitalists for Germany's woes. Support for the Nazi Party increased and by 1932 it was the largest in the *Reichstag* (Parliament). The election of the next year was a travesty. Joseph Goebbels turned the press and radio stations into pro-Nazi organisations, whilst brown-shirted militia men beat anyone who defied them. Unsurprisingly, Hitler was triumphant. Communist deputies were arrested by the Gestapo, stormtroopers surrounded the *Reichstag* and apart from the Socialists all the parties voted for Hitler to become dictator.

Benito Mussolini, Il Duce of Italy.

This event signalled an onslaught against those loathed by the Nazis. Laws were enacted which allowed the mass sterilisation of people who were declared to have genetic, mental, physical or social defects. Homosexuality became a crime and Romanies were persecuted. Jews as well as those with Jewish ancestry were expelled from the civil service. All other political parties were disbanded, independent trade unions were stamped out and communist leaders were forced into newly-established concentration camps such as Dachau. In May 1933 there were shocking scenes when books by Jewish and anti-Nazi writers were piled up in public places and set on fire. Two years later the first of the Nuremberg Laws were passed. These included obscene definitions of race which made Jews inferior to Aryans, the term used by Hitler to define blond-haired, blue-eyed, Nordic looking people. Marriages between the two groups were forbidden and a Jewish man could be executed for having sex with an Aryan.

There were only 500,000 German Jews and the great majority were like Henry Warner - they saw themselves as good citizens.

> *We were very, very German. We went to the Synagogue occasionally, and held a Seder at Passover, but not much else. We were sure the highly civilised German people would not put up with Hitler for long, and when we woke up - it was too late.*
> (Zoë Josephs, *Survivors. Jewish Refugees in Birmingham 1933-1945*, Oldbury, 1988, p. 11).

Hitler and his supporters ignored the allegiances of the German Jews, forcing Henry and others to flee from bigotry. Those Jews who stayed were put under increasing restrictions, losing their rights and their jobs. On 9 November 1938 a pogrom was launched against them. It was known as *Kristallnacht*, the night of the crystals, because so much glass shattered onto the streets of Berlin as Nazis smashed the windows of Jewish businesses. Synagogues were set ablaze, Jewish homes were broken into and their occupants assaulted to the shouts of *Judah verrecke* - 'perish the Jew'.

Such actions were apparent elsewhere in Germany. Living in a small town on the border with Czechoslovakia, Charlotte Singer was woken abruptly by the clatter of china and the shouts of a large crowd. In her room stood one of her husband's patients. Wielding a hatchet he destroyed whatever he could: 'the furniture was broken in a few seconds, my writing table was overturned, ink dripping on to the carpet'. Then a brick was hurled through the window, hitting Charlotte's leg, and 'another evil-looking crowd, women among them, wrecked the kitchen'. (Josephs, *Survivors*, p. 20). This havoc and fright were welcomed by the Nazi leadership. Joseph Goebbels wrote in his diary that the *Führer* had decided that the 'Jews should be made to feel the wrath of the people. He went on, 'as I head for the hotel, I see the sky is blood-red. The synagogue is burning'. (J.A.S. Grenville, *The Collins History of the World in the Twentieth Century* , London, 1994, p. 237. John Grenville himself was a young Jewish refugee from Germany.)

Hitler's racial policies were not adopted in Italy until after the outbreak of the Second World War, but nearby in Austria many people believed in them and on 12 March 1938 German troops marched across the frontier. There was no opposition and a day later the two countries were united in the *Anschluss*. It seemed that in only one place could the march of fascism be halted - Spain. In 1936 civil war had broken out there when a number of generals led their troops in revolt against the democratically-elected government. Eventually led by Franco, the army gathered to it conservatives of every kind - as well as members of the fascist Falange. They were opposed by republicans, socialists, anarchists, communists and Catholic Basque and Catalan nationalists. As with Hitler and Mussolini, Franco took on a personal title - *El Caudillo* - and he made much use of blue-shirted falangists. Cruel acts were committed on both sides, and each was supported by outside powers. Germany supplied the insurgents with fighter planes, bombers, tanks and anti-aircraft guns as well as experts and the 5,000 men of the Condor Legion. Italy also

The burning of books regarded by the Nazis as Jewish, 'degenerate' and 'un-German', May 1933.

Hitler surrounded by Nazis at the third rally of his party in Nuremburg, 1927.

provided aircraft and tanks as well as motor vehicles, machine guns, flame throwers, rifles, artillery, ammunition, bombs and tens of thousands of men. More than this, Italian warships and submarines attacked Republican shipping.

The Soviets did not send soldiers to help the Republic but did give significant military assistance via advisers, tanks and planes. They also organised the International Brigades, volunteers from across Europe and North America. The feelings of many of these men were summed up by Ted Smallbone, a communist from Cotteridge, Birmingham:

> *I could only see the Spain affair as one in which the Germans and the Italians were establishing another Fascist state to give them the strength to fight Communism. And this was the overriding thing at the time - if Spain got defeated in its attempts to become a democratic country, and then did become a Fascist dictatorship, I couldn't see anything other than a major European war breaking out.* (Howard Williamson, *Toolmaking and Politics. The life of Ted Smallbone - an oral history*, Birmingham, 1987, p. 42).

For Hitler and the Nazis, Spain was a place where they could test weaponry, tactics and the terrorisation of a civilian population. This was shown graphically on Monday 26 April 1937 when Guernica in the Basque Country was blitzed by German bombers. The attack was signalled at 4.30 p.m. when the church bells began to peal in warning. Guernica was filled with its own folk, refugees and those drawn in by the market. As Heinkels launched their destructive and deathful loads, these defenceless people were machine gunned from Messerschmitts. According to G.L. Steer, a journalist with *The London Mercury*:

> *On the shattered houses, whose carpets and curtains, splintered beams and floors and furniture were knocked into angles and ready for the burning, the planes threw*

silver flakes. Tubes of two pounds, long as your forearm, glistening silver from their aluminium and elektron casing: inside them, as in the beginning of the world in Prometheus' reed, slept fire. Fire in a silver powder, sixty-five grammes in weight, ready to slip through six holes at the base of the glittering tube. So as the houses were broken to pieces over the people sheathed fire descended from heaven to burn them up. (Valentine Cunningham, ed, *Spanish Front. Writers on the Civil War*, Oxford 1986, p. 134)

Forty-three aircraft were involved in the raid, which lasted three hours. They dropped 100,000 tons of high explosives, incendiaries and shrapnel bombs. Perhaps 1,000 people were slaughtered and many more were maimed and wounded. Guernica was a bitter foretaste of the Blitz on Britain and elsewhere.

The Spanish Civil War ended in March 1939 when Madrid capitulated to Franco's men. By now a great and terrible European conflict seemed likely. Since coming to power Hitler had swiftly rearmed Germany, reintroduced conscription and given priority to building up the nation's war industries. He had actively backed Franco and had not been gainsaid by the United Kingdom, France and the United States of America; in 1936 these countries had not prevented him from sending the *Wehrmacht* into the Rhineland - German territory which had been demilitarised after the First World War; they had not stopped him when he forcibly united Austria with Germany; and in October 1938 they had acquiesced in his take-over of the Sudetenland, a part of Czechoslovakia where many Germans lived. Chamberlain and Daladier, the Prime Ministers of the United Kingdom and France, had agreed to Germany's move with Hitler and Mussolini at a conference in Munich. In return the *Führer* had signed a statement that from then on all disputes between the United Kingdom and Germany would be settled diplomatically. Brummie Hilda Daw recalled Chamberlain's triumphant return to the airport, as he waved the treaty in his hand and declared he had secured. 'Peace in our time'. She was not convinced,

Neville Chamberlain, Prime Minister of the United Kingdom, on his return from Munich and waving his agreement with Hitler, September 1938.

wondering 'who would believe the great dictator's aspirations to be honourable?' Tragically her doubts were realised and Chamberlain's high expectations were dashed. (Letter, 29.6.96).

Throughout the 1930s appeasement of this kind had been the main policy of the major democracies towards Hitler's Germany. There were a number of reasons why such diplomacy was preferred to a military solution. First, France was riven with dissension between left and right and was enfeebled further by a succession of short-lived and impotent governments. Second, despite President Roosevelt's wishes, the Congress of the United States of America was determinedly isolationist and vehemently wanted to steer clear of involvement in Europe. And third, led by Stanley Baldwin and then Neville Chamberlain, the United Kingdom was preoccupied with domestic policy. The focus was on improving the economy, and at a time of Depression it was felt that spending money on arms would worsen the nation's financial situation. There were other considerations. Many people believed that there was some justification to the take-overs of the Sudetenland and Austria because Germany had been treated harshly at the end of the First World War. This conflict had been so violent that most British politicians were avowed in their intent that it should not be repeated. They were prepared to do as much as they could diplomatically to maintain peace. Finally, the British armed forces were unprepared for a conflict, and their meagre resources were stretched by the need to defend India and Australia from potential Japanese aggression. Winston Churchill was one of the few politicians of stature who warned against the policy of appeasement. He went unheeded. The political and public mood was for peace. Few people believed that Hitler was intent on expansionism and war. They were disabused as the fragile European peace crumbled at the waning of the 1930s.

Hitler was not pacified by his successes. Instead he was encouraged by the lack of firm action against him. Demoralised by the lack of support from the United Kingdom and France and intimidated by threats of bombing, in early March 1939 the Czech President signed over the independence of his country. British public opinion was outraged. At the end of the month Chamberlain authorised a doubling in strength of the Territorial Army and he agreed a unilateral guarantee with France whereby both nations would defend Poland and Romania from any German offensives. The position of the allies was made more difficult in May by the Pact of Steel between Hitler and Mussolini. On 23 August it deteriorated further with the conclusion of a surprising Non-Aggression Pact between the USSR and the communist-hating Nazi Germany. Freed from the concern of a major threat, Hitler determined to conquer Poland. His ultimate aims were to subjugate all non-Aryan races like the Slavic Poles and to make *Lebensraum*. This was 'living space' - land in the east which would be 'racially cleansed' so that Germans could settle there and increase in numbers.

Throughout August the Nazis pressurised the Poles to cede territory. Steadfastly they resisted, boosted by a stiffening of the resolves of France and the United Kingdom. In a personal letter to Hitler it was emphasised by Chamberlain that the British would stand by their guarantees, and on 25 August a formal Anglo-Polish alliance was agreed. It stated that the United Kingdom would go to war if Poland were attacked by Germany. The same day Mussolini told Hitler that Italy did not have the resources for an outright European conflict. These events were followed by much diplomatic toing and froing in an almost frantic attempt to preserve the peace. Such efforts were in vain. At 4.45 a.m. on 1 September Poland was invaded by Germany. Two days later the United Kingdom and France sent ultimatums to Hitler demanding the withdrawal of his forces from Poland. They were ignored and war was declared.

The sombreness of the occasion was remembered by Ray Pegg:

> When the war broke out I was 11 years old. Everyone had been told to listen to the radio at 11 am on Sunday morning Sept 3rd. The Prime Minister Neville Chamberlain began by telling us that he was speaking from the 'Kibinit' room and ended by saying that as the Germans had not replied to his note, we were now at war with them. Everyone was thunderstruck and went into a dazed silence. I remember breaking this by giving a nervous laugh, wherein my elder sister with a black look on her face smacked me across the ear. We all then went outside to find that the sky was full of Barrage Balloons, grey and menacing. (Letter 21.2.95)

Frances Winstanley had similar feelings. She lived with her aunt in Upper Sutton Street, Aston and the morning of 1 September she was shampooing her hair. A towel draped over her shoulders, the 'furthest thing from my mind just then was the war'. Her thoughts were concentrated on whether or not she should have her hair cut. Standing up, she twiddled the knobs on the 'old battery-run wireless set' and heard 'the grave voice of Neville Chamberlain'. Gone were the hopeful tones of the previous September when the Prime Minister had returned from Munich. With 'terror striking at my heart' Frances ran into the next room where her aunt and cousin were

German troops entering Hradcany Castle, Prague, the seat of the Czechoslovakian President, March 1939.

in tears. As they cried, her brother Les 'stood informing anyone who was willing to listen, how powerful were the modern bombs, but by way of comfort how little you would know of it if you were hit by one'. Within days, Les had joined the army and soon after Frances was directed to 'a new war-work job at the General Electric Company in Witton'. (Frances Winstanley, *Sparrers Can't Sing*, Birmingham, 1991, pp. 150-1).

Diplomatic efforts to preserve peace had been futile. At last the British and French had realised that Hitler could not be appeased. His objective was to control Europe and he intended to do so by crushing one nation at a time. Once the small states had been overcome then he would have turned against the United Kingdom and France. Better to fight now than to wait until most of Europe was cowed by the Germans. It can never be a good thing to go to war. But there can be little doubt that on 3 September 1939 the United Kingdom and France did the right thing by declaring war and resisting Hitler's aggression against Poland. The Poles fought valiantly both against the Germans and the Soviets, who had launched an attack from the east on 17 September. Ten days later the Polish defenders of Warsaw surrendered to the *Wehrmacht* and the Nazis began to implement their wicked racial policies. Poles were treated as slaves. As the vanquished, they had to defer to their conquerors at all times, moving off the pavements and doffing their hats. Young women with 'nordic' looks were forced into *Lebensborn*, human stud farms where they were compelled to have sex with SS men so that the 'master race' could be bred. And Jews were humiliated, beaten, driven out of their homes and businesses and killed.

With the fall of Poland hostilities switched to the sea and there was a lull in the war on the land. The Poles had inflicted heavy losses on the enemy and the Nazis were not ready to switch their attention to the western front, whilst the French were unprepared to assault the German Siegfried Line and instead mobilised behind their own fortifications, the Maginot Line. They were supported by a British Expeditionary Force which was stationed along the Belgian frontier. For his part, Chamberlain believed that an economic blockade would lead Hitler to the negotiating table. This 'phoney war' lasted for seven months. In the United Kingdom it was a time of preparation for the armed forces and the civilian authorities. All the major cities made ready to withstand air raids. Birmingham was no exception.

Great Days

Nineteen-thirty nine and the world has changed,
My own little life has been rearranged.
Gas masks issued to all and sundry,
Seemed like a game till one fateful Monday.
Mother told me to be strong, not to worry,
But into their shelters the people all scurry,
The Luftwaffe flew a deafening blitz,
And blew my childhood homes to bits.
Listening to the wireless set at the home of a friend,
Sounds as if the war has reached its joyous end.
I remember the drink flowed, hoarded whisky and rum,
The night peace fell over our beloved Brummagem.

Edith Fishgutter

CHAPTER ONE

BRUM STAYS CALM:
AIR RAID PRECAUTIONS

Women air raid wardens, reporting for duty.

No Blank Cheque: the Cost of A.R.P.

Vivid news film of the conflicts in Spain, Abyssinia and China brought to the British people the awfulness of modern warfare. Hostilities of any kind had always been horrifying, but the conflicts of the 1930s seemed worse because they enveloped in pain and suffering not only servicemen but also huge numbers of civilians. This was an unprecedented shift in warfare. Distressing footage showed the panic of old men, women and children as they fled air raids and the onslaughts of enemy troops. It conveyed graphically the distraught expressions, the grieving faces and the wearied looks. It made plain the gruesome injuries, the ghastly maimings and the grisly corpses. It revealed clearly the maliciousness, cruelty and destructiveness of the victors and the despair, hopelessness and sorrow of the defeated. It stressed the havoc, the desolation and the inhumanity of war. It highlighted that war could never be glamorous, that war contorted, warped and disfigured lives, minds, spirits and places.

The effects of aerial bombing in particular affected the considerations of the British government. As early as 1935, when appeasement was pursued vigorously and rearmament was still resisted, procedures were put in place for training experts who could co-ordinate civilian responses if war broke out and there were raids on Britain's cities. A circular about 'Air Raid Precautions' (A.R.P.) was sent out to councils, encouraging them to co-operate with Westminster and private employers to set up local A.R.P. organisations. The public were urged to join such bodies. Primarily the government was concerned that municipalities should provide an adequate emergency ambulance service and facilities for training in anti-gas procedures. Although Birmingham Corporation appointed a special committee to deal with the government's proposals, its overall response was dilatory. One person who sought to activate his fellow councillors was Norman Tiptaft. In 1936 he visited Germany and saw the serious manner in

'Warship Week' poster on the side of the Town Hall, urging Brummies to donate enough money to buy a warship, 18 October 1941. The poster was believed to be the biggest in the world and was the work of Robert Johnson of Erdington, an employee in the advertising department at Joseph Lucas Ltd.

which the Nazis treated civil defence. He returned to Birmingham 'hoping to rouse my fellow citizens, if not my country; but most of the City Fathers regarded A.R.P. as a waste of money'. The next year he became chairman of the A.R.P. Committee and was given the services of a part-time officer and a typist. Together 'we were supposed to ensure Birmingham's safety in case of air raids - not, of course, that such a thing was even thought remotely possible'. (Norman Tiptaft, *The Individualist*, Birmingham, 1954, p. 168).

Battling against 'public and private apathy' Tiptaft's difficulties were compounded by financial concerns. As late as March 1939, when war seemed imminent, the chairperson of the Finance Committee, Alderman S. J. Grey, declared that 'the international position does not mean a blank cheque for A.R.P. - not even for petty cash'. After hostilities began such considerations remained uppermost in the minds of many elected representatives, leading Tiptaft to express his dissatisfaction with statements made about spending on A.R.P. He explained that 'no definite instance of extravagance was given, but vague and general charges - like "colossal waste" and "expenditure that would stagger the council if known" - were made'. It was accusations such as these which have led Anthony Sutcliffe and Roger Smith to argue that 'the City Council was extremely unsympathetic to the needs of civil defence'.

('A.R.P. Committee and its Critics', *Birmingham Post*, 13 November 1939; Anthony Sutcliffe and Roger Smith, *History of Birmingham. Volume III. Birmingham 1939-1970*, Oxford, 1974, p. 18).

There can be no doubt that taking precautions for air raids was expensive. By January 1940 the city was spending £5,000 a day on A.R.P. Totalling the huge sum of £1,800,000 a year, a fifth of this amount was met via the rates (the forerunner of the Council Tax), whilst the greater part was paid for by the government. Such figures did not take into account the value of equipment supplied from Westminster, and it excluded the costs of evacuation and of the emergency hospitals schemes. At the same time as outgoings were increasing, the council had to face 'the considerable potential loss of income due to the war, e.g. evacuation of dwelling-houses and offices, loss of profits in the case of business enterprises, and what may prove to be even more important, the destruction of property as a result enemy air raids'.

('Birmingham Defence', *Birmingham Mail*, 4 January 1940).

To pay for the war effort the council raised the rates, whilst the government increased income tax and from January 1940 sold National Savings Certificates and Defence Bonds. These were expensive and as a result many people pooled their money to buy them. Throughout Birmingham such groups were formed in factories, offices and neighbourhoods. One tireless worker in selling National Savings Certificates was Nora Bedford.

In 1942 I became ward organiser for Kingstanding, Gt Barr & Pheasey Estate. Apart from running a street group which we looked after & supplying equipment and selling from door to door stamps and certificates, we canvassed all the streets and also those of other organisers all over the city. We would first appeal door to door for members and having gained a quarter would seek one to take charge of that group and leave a credit stock of £10, to carry on. Although these duties were carried out at night in the blackout I never once remember being afraid. I had 65

The Lord Mayor, Alderman Martineau, and the Lady Mayoress riding a tank in a parade to encourage women to enlist for war work, 6 September 1941.

secretaries working and during the annual big weeks 'Salute the Soldier' 'Wings for Victory' everyone would rally together to run events like concerts, Exhibition dances, Whist drives etc. I begged prizes from local shops to present as prizes for the best selling efforts. (Letter, 24 February 1995).

By 5 November 1940, there were 3,566 savings groups in Birmingham. With individuals and companies they had bought National Savings Certificates totalling £22,233,149 - the equivalent of just over £21 per person. At the end of the war the number of savings groups had swollen to between 6,000 and 7,000. ('Birmingham's War Weapons Week', *Birmingham Post*, 5 November 1940).

There were other initiatives to raise money. In 1940 a Spitfire Fund collected £4,387, including a donation of £75 made by children at Golden Hillock Road Junior and Infant Schools; and on 14 October of that year a War Weapons Week was launched at Baskerville House by Clementine Churchill, the wife of the new Prime Minister. There were similar drives in Liverpool, Manchester and Bradford, and all featured march-pasts by soldiers and sailors. Locally, it was aimed to collect £8,000,000 and to lend the money to the nation through the purchase of Bonds and National Savings Certificates. The sum would pay for the equivalent of 250 bombers and 600 fighters. June Picken remembered the occasion. She worked as a Holerith machine operator at Stewart's and Lloyd's in Easy Row. Their premises overlooked the car park of the 'West End' picture house where many of the servicemen gathered before their marching began.

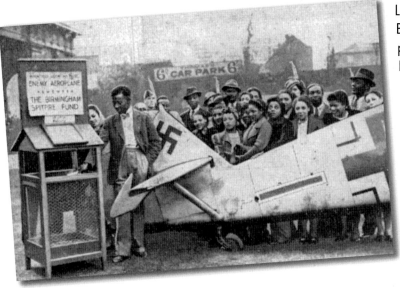

Black actors from 'various parts of the British Empire' performing at the Theatre Royal, New Street and turning up to support cash-raising efforts for the Spitfire Fund, 23 September 1940.

Little did we know how poorly off Britain was for weapons. Disarmament had been relentlessly carried out in the 30s despite warnings from ex-servicemen like my Dad about the growth of Nazism. The young soldiers, on seeing girls' faces looking down on them, endeavoured to make dates, writing on pieces of paper and wrapping the paper round a stone, throwing it up to the girl of their fancy. Our floor was too high up for such goings on, we were content to watch! (Letter, 8 July 1996).

The response was enthusiastic and contributions ranged from the £800,000 given by the Britannic Assurance to the £130 raised by 200 pupils at Osler Street School, Ladywood. Over the week the total brought in was £8,150,000. A year later the focus of attention was a 'Warship Week' which raised the even bigger amount of £10,088,919. This was the cost of a battleship and meant that the city 'won the distinction of "adopting"' the George V. Although Glasgow substantially bettered this sum, 40% of Birmingham's amount was from members of the working class. The amount subscribed by the little investors of Brum was 34s 7d (£1.73p) per head compared to 21s 5½d (£1.07) per head in Glasgow. In small contributions the city was 'far ahead of any other place in the country'. Working-class Brummies continued their fine record during 'Wings for Victory Week' in July 1943. Two years later it was declared that 'no other town or city in England reached Birmingham's per capita figure' in savings. ('Weapons Week', *Birmingham Mail*, 15 October 1940; 'Warship Week in Birmingham', *Birmingham Post*, 29 October 1941; 'Small Investors' Fine Achievement', *Birmingham Weekly Post*, 21 November 1941; 'Wings for Victory Week', *Birmingham Post*, 9 July 1943; . 'Small Savings Record', *Birmingham Post Supplement*, 8 May 1945).

A Strange Time: Preparing for Air Raids

Most municipal departments spent money on Civil Defence, but the bulk of the cost was incurred by the A.R.P. Committee. Spurred on by the worsening situation on the continent, in 1938 this had been elected as a standing committee to the council with its headquarters in Broad Street. Tiptaft admitted in his memoirs that the most difficult aspect about preparing for war 'was that nobody knew what to do'. There were no precedents, although in the First World War zeppelin raids had been made on the United Kingdom. Now the nation had to make ready for the possibility of sustained heavy bombing from the air. In these circumstances everyone had his or her ideas about what were the

An example of the new National Identity cards, a green card with a photograph and a description of the holder, 13 January 1940.

correct procedures. Unsurprisingly, there was indecision, there were mistakes and there was muddle. Yet 'somehow, something else did get done, and organisations of the loosest possible kind, with the minimum of expert knowledge and the maximum of red tape, came into being'. (Tiptaft, *The Individualist*, pp. 174-5; 'How the A.R.P. Service was Evolved, *Birmingham Post*, 10 February 1940).

From 1 September 1939 A.R.P. activities and the overall running of Birmingham were supervised by an Emergency Powers Committee. Its members included the Lord Mayor, Alderman Sir Ernest Canning, Aldermen Byng Kenrick and Harold Roberts and Councillor Tiptaft. The Town Clerk, Sir Frank Wiltshire, was made the city's Wartime Controller. Tiptaft recollected that 'one terribly tiring night in the winter of

1940', Sir Frank received information that his house in Wellington Road, Edgbaston had been bombed. Not knowing 'what had happened to his wife and the members of his household, his fortitude in carrying on without any visible reaction to that message will be remembered by all who were with him that night'. (Tiptaft, *The Individualist*, p. 183). Fortunately, the Wiltshires survived.

The Wartime Controller worked from a fortified basement in the Council House. This was in direct contact with nine report centres elsewhere in the city. Each was well-protected, gas-proofed and had two sets of staff. They included a message supervisor, plotters of maps, telephonists, filing clerks and messengers - all recruited from professionals. They were headed by a controlling officer who was a corporation official. Above the city authorities was the Earl of Dudley, the Regional A.R.P. Commissioner for the Midlands. He was appointed by the Home Office and had his headquarters in Birmingham. Within the city there was one other essential point of command - the War Room, a deep, well-protected basement at the main police station. This was the nerve centre of police and civil defence operations during air raids. At all times it was attended by the Chief Constable, or one of his Assistants, and by liaison officers from both the military in the region and National Fire Service. It had an Information Room which gave radio connection to control stations as well as police stations and cars, and it provided a means of communication and co-ordination with neighbouring police forces.

Ambulance drivers having a cup of tea in a 24 hour canteen for A.R.P. workers at the depot in Court Road, Sparkhill, 27 October 1939.

On the ground the operations of A.R.P. were helped by 300 trainers, some of whom had received instruction at Home Office bases. At a local training school in Kings Norton they worked with A.R.P. volunteers, whose numbers swelled to 55,000 people within a fortnight of the outbreak of war. As one reporter stressed 'this by no means exhausts the number of citizens who are rendering public service', for there were also hundreds of men and women who were engaged in social service work and were not attached to an official body. Everybody seemed to be doing something to prepare for bombing raids. Clergymen attended lessons in first-aid given by members of the St John's Ambulance Brigade. Teachers explained to children how to put on gas masks and how to make their way to air raid shelters. Thousands of people gave blood. Members of the Boy's Brigade were enrolled as messengers who could take casualty lists from hospitals to a central issuing office. Girl Guides became nurses, A.R.P. wardens or worked with the Women's Voluntary Service - an organisation which

Schoolboys in a non-evacuated area helping to fill sandbags to protect their school, which was turned into a temporary hospital and clearing station, 1 September 1939.

operated canteens in A.R.P. depots like those at Rose Road, Harborne and Court Road, Sparkhill. Boy Scouts went around collecting waste paper for the war effort and became blood donors. The Y.M.C.A. started to operate mobile canteens for A.R.P. workers. And the Salvation Army went about collecting for its vital work at home and abroad. ('Solid Home Front', *Birmingham Mail*, 15 September 1939).

Everywhere there was evidence of preparations for war. To keep the city hidden from enemy bombers, a blackout was imposed each evening and windows were covered with dark paper or material. The Town Hall, Council House and other major buildings were protected by walls of sandbags. Victoria Square was dotted with black and yellow flags which pointed the way to public air raid shelters. Strips of gummed paper were stuck to shop windows to try and stop the glass from shattering outwards if there was bombing nearby. Boxes filled with sandbags covered the gratings and skylights in places like Colonnade Passage, New Street. People walked about with gas masks trailing from boxes attached to their waists, and at night they held small torches to light their way in sombre streets. Parks were ploughed and made ready for growing food. Posters urged people to make do and mend. Announcements in the newspapers told folk about the rationing system. Saucepans were handed in to help make Spitfires. Salvage bins were placed on streets, for the deposit of paper, bones and metal. And A. R. P. volunteers engaged in 'realistic exercises' in parks and roads. They rescued 'casualties' from damaged buildings; they put out mock blazes; they dealt with incendiary bombs in specially constructed tin huts; they made trial runs from their depots to check the time it took to cover their district; and they practised decontamination routines.

A number of things struck Mrs N. Williams about the changed look of things. People 'all seemed stunned and yet there was a determination to do what we were told & we did'. She put gas masks on her children and walked them 'around the table to get used to them, not very pleasant'. But what impressed her most was 'the strangeness of it when I arrived at the Swan Yardley & saw this huge thing like an elephant floating in the sky'. It was a barrage balloon, sent aloft to hinder enemy aircraft, and its presence heralded 'that life would be different'. (Letter, 22 February 1995). Six years old at the time, Bill Quinney of Millward Street, Small Heath also realised that his world was transforming. He was aware of his parents listening to news bulletins 'and the fact that we children had to keep quiet'. He recognised the sandbags, the gas masks and the Anderson Shelters. He noticed that when he was out with his parents 'we would see a queue outside a shop and on asking what the queue

Registering for petrol ration books at the Birmingham Motor Taxation Office, 15 September 1939.

was for would join it as perhaps the shop had just had a delivery of something and even the shops were limited to their stock'. He saw the erection of shelters, the closure of the local swimming baths at Green Lane, and the appearance of water tanks. And he looked on as his father joined the A.R.P. (Letter, 17 April 1995).

Duty and Bravery: Air Raid Wardens

A major feature of civil defence was the Air Raid Wardens' Service, which peaked at 19,800 members - most of whom were part-timers. Headed at first by the Chief Constable and then by a Chief Warden, by early 1940 they were distinguished by their uniforms and helmets. Six or more of them were headed by a senior warden and each team, split into day and night shifts, was charged with a sector of 500 people. In total there were 2,303 sectors and 450 posts. These were run both by paid wardens and by those who were volunteer clerks, telephonists and messengers. The posts served about five sectors and were chosen for their strategic significance. At the outbreak of war they were reinforced by well-protected action posts. ('Birmingham's Air Raid Wardens Service', *Birmingham Post*, 21 October 1939).

In 1940 Pat Evans was a twelve-year old living in Alum Rock. Both her mom and dad joined the A.R.P.:

> and our frontroom was called sector 6. On a table were a bell, rattle and a board which turned a different colour if there was gas around. As soon as the sirens sounded Mom & Dad went on duty, leaving me with the first person they met with in a shelter, not knowing where I was till after the raid . . . Mom joined the ARP as a

paid warden when they moved into Nansen Road school. When she was on duty I spent any free time there. I saw Coventry burning, also with sadness watched the digging, trying to save my friends, 2 little brothers whose father had been killed when a bomb landed on their house, only for them to be gassed when a pipe was fractured at the corner of Highfield Road. When we lost all our windows in Kimberley Avenue we moved to my Nan's at Gowan Road, only to have an incendiary bomb burn out our front bedroom. Mom was on the Post at the time and answered the call. (Letter, July 1995).

Margaret Cooper's dad was 'Chief Air Raid Warden' for his sector and 'kept the Roster Book wherein the men on duty that night signed on'. When there was no raid, 'as they'd already been to work and were tired it was decided that I would take the book to the men who were on duty and they could sign without another unnecessary walk'. For her efforts, Margaret was paid a 1d by each man and 'I bought my first Children's Encyclopaedia from our local newsagents with that money'. (Letter, 24 February 1995).

From the late 1930s wardens had received a mass of material telling them how they should act in certain situations. Living in Copthall Road, Handsworth, Mr A.B. Berry was Head Air Raid Warden of the Holyhead Road Sub-Division, Group C. During the Blitz, a colleague stated that he was 'always on the spot' when needed. ('Houses Damaged', *Birmingham Mail*, 12 March 1941). After the war his wife, Madge, kept a great variety of the information that was sent to them concerning air raid precautions, civil defence and the wardens' service. Now deposited in the City Archives at Birmingham Central Library, collection MS1346 has circulars, notes, forms, stationery, air raid log books, report forms on air raid damage, record books of the sector fire parties and air raid wardens in C26, maps, the minute books of Housewives Service Group C2639, lists of alerts and 47 publications. These

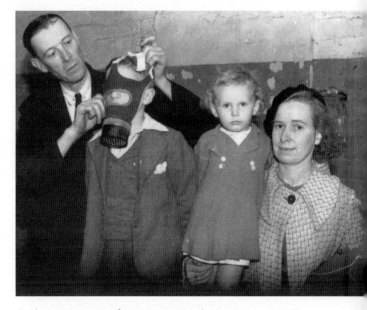

A demonstration in fitting a gas mask, 26 August 1939.

latter were issued by the Home Office (Air Raid Precautions Department), the Ministry of Home Security, the Lord Privy Seal's Office, the Ministry of Information, the City of Birmingham and miscellaneous bodies such as the Canned Foods Advisory Bureau and the Institution of Gas Engineers. The leaflets, pamphlets and booklets range from 'Notes for the guidance of wardens at rescue incidents' to 'Fire Guard Instruction No. 1. The fire guard plan', and from 'The use of reserve food stores' to 'Notes on town gas for air raid wardens'.

The Berry Archive highlights the numerous responsibilities of wardens. They ensured that people observed the blackout, they were trained in anti-gas measures, they handed out gas masks and demonstrated their use, and from May 1940 they fitted

A.R.P. workers at a bomb site in Bridge Street West, off Summer Lane, 30 July 1942.

respirators with an improved filter. Most importantly, wardens had to be on duty when air raids threatened. If there was an attack they were to direct citizens to air raid shelters and rest centres, put out incendiary bombs, report any incidents, assist the appropriate rescue and medical services, and keep people calm. Great bravery was shown by wardens, amongst them Mr B. Rogers. He lived at 33 Hams Road, Saltley and was A.R.P. for the road:

> *There were many raids in Autumn 1941. One night I was on duty, the air-raid warning was given and the fire bombers came over dropping their loads of fire bombs. The anti aircraft guns opened up. The search lights flashed all around indicating a heavy raid. I made a quick check along the road. I spotted a fire starting up in a front bed room. I ran in upstairs, threw bedclothes and bomb through the window, saving the house & possibly the road. The bombers then arrived dropping the heavy bombs. I had to go into the shelter for a time. After the all clear, there were fires burning all around.* (Letter, 1 May 1995).

Similar courage was shown by Amelia Johnston, of Ravenshurst Street, Camp Hill. She was on patrol duty when she realised that eight people were trapped in a wrecked house. Despite the falling bombs and heavy ack-ack fire, 'she went to the first-aid post, directed a doctor to the scene, and tried to get through the debris into the cellar'. Unable to achieve her objective, she fetched a rescue party and helped attend the casualties. She was awarded the British Empire Medal, and it was believed that she was 'Britain's first woman warden' to gain this distinction. ('Hospital Heroes', *Birmingham Mail*, 5 July 1941). Amelia was not the only gallant woman. Another was Beatrice Withers, a shopkeeper from Balsall Heath. One night in November 1940 she was on duty in St Paul's Road, paying particular attention to a woman, who was on the verge of blood poisoning, and who had a baby with her. Two bombs dropped on a nearby house and Beatrice was hit in the temple by four pieces of shrapnel, whilst pieces of glass and a window frame 'came flying over me'. Recovering, she blew her whistle, called for help and went to rescue the mother and baby. This she did. Then she moved to the house which had taken the full force of the explosives, recalling that 'I shall never forget the sight'. The building was wrecked and it seemed that no-one could have survived the frightful blast.

> *Suddenly we heard a child's faint whimper. Rescue men who came on the scene started tunnelling from the next door cellar and soon saw a woman's hands sticking out towards them. I said, 'That must be Mrs Sharp. The baby will be near.' This proved to be true. The mother had been sitting around the kitchen fire with her children, and when the bomb came and blew them and the fire grate as well into the cellar below she had the mother's instinct to throw herself protectingly over her youngest - Marjorie aged five and a half. The little one was unhurt and soon opened her eyes. Mrs Sharp just idolised that kid. She is a grand little girl, with flaxen hair and dark brown eyes.* ('Very Bad Night', *Birmingham Mail*, 28 March 1941).

Usually the family went to a shelter but they had stayed at home because Mrs Edith Sharp had a heavy cold. She was killed by the bomb, as were three of her children from her first marriage - Frederick, Raymond and Joyce Carey. Also killed were Jessie, John and Dennis Sharp whilst their father, Alfred, died a month later of his injuries. Bob White was the rescuer who dug out Marjorie, the survivor. He was just sixteen-years old. In 1980 his account was published in an *Evening Mail Special*. A relative sent it to Marjorie Sharp, who was now married and living in Newport, Shropshire. She wrote to the man who had saved her life, thanking him 'for the happiness that I have enjoyed in the years that have passed' since the raid. On 10 December 1980 they met and for the first time since the bomb fell, Marjorie went back to St Paul's Road. Later in the war Bob White was awarded the Distinguished Flying Cross for his courage as a Lancaster tailgunner. ('Plucked from the jaws of death', *Evening Mail Special. November 1940*, November 1980; 'At last, Marjorie meets the man who saved her young life', *Evening Mail*, 10 December 1980, thanks to Nancy White).

Beatrice Withers was made an Officer of the Order of the British Empire, whilst Charles Arthur Freeman was awarded the George Medal. A voluntary warden from Cooksey Road, Small Heath he rushed to two houses which had been blown up. With his hands he burrowed beneath the rubble and recovered two bodies. As he did so 'debris overhung the spot, there was a strong escape of gas, and high explosive bombs and shrapnel from A.A.

Olive Perry, ambulance driver/attendant. Her mother, Gladys Gisbourne, and other A.R.P. workers were trapped under a girder when bombs hit the Public Works Department Depot in Kings Road, Tyseley. They were saved and taken to the Casualty Clearing Station at Church Road, Yardley.

guns were falling'. At the same ceremony attended by George, Winifred Yate of Gopsal Street, Duddeston was honoured with the British Empire Medal. She had assisted in leading 200 heavy dray horses from stables which adjoined burning premises. One animal stepped on her foot and injured it, 'but she remained on duty until the "Raiders Passed" sounded'. A few days later Winifred rescued two men injured by falling debris, after which an explosion hurt her so badly that she had to spend three months in hospital. (''Bravery in Raids', *Birmingham Mail*, 14 June 1941). Sixteen other wardens received British Empire Medals and eleven were commended by the King. Seventy-seven of their comrades were killed by the enemy and 414 were injured. On 4 September 1941, the growth and prestige of the A.R.P. services were recognised when the organisation was renamed Civil Defence. ('"C.D." Instead of "A.R.P."', *Birmingham Mail*, 4 September 1941).

Fighting Flames: the Fire Services

In 1936 the Home Office had pressed Birmingham to adopt a fire protection scheme for the city, on the assumption that within a few minutes a concerted air raid could lead to an outbreak of 1,000 blazes. In coping with such a conflagration, a major worry was the need for substantial amounts of water. The city's supply came from the Elan Valley in Wales, where armed guards were placed. On its journey the water was carried over six bridges and it entered the city at just one point. A direct hit at any of these places could dangerously disrupt the flow of water at a time of raids. It was apparent that stand-by supplies were vital and plans were laid for raising the levels of canals and the River Rea. Other contingencies included the delivery of hundreds of rectangular metal storage tanks and river pumps; the construction of five miles of piping in the city centre for the relaying of water if the mains were fractured; and the laying of a 24 inch water main between Dudley Road and Newhall Street.

As important as an uninterrupted supply of water was a large body of men who could combat flames. Full-time firemen would need to be supported by volunteers and in July 1937 an Auxiliary Fire Service (A.F.S.) was formed. By early 1940 it had 10,000 members, 4,000 of whom were fully trained ('Civic Defence', *Birmingham Mail*, 1 January 1940). This compared to 300 regular firemen. There was opposition to the new body and the Chief Officer of the Fire Brigade refused to allow his officers to work with the volunteers. This position began to change in January 1940 when one regular was transferred to each A.F.S. station. Still the volunteers were headed by their own officers, most of whom were businessmen, and about a fifth of the A.F.S. members were full-timers. The force included men who were firefighters and those who were on station and telephone duty; women who were telephonists and despatch riders; and boys who were messengers. One of these was the fifteen-year old Bob Steadman. Along with his mates Ted, Bert and Fred they worked during the day and each night split into two teams for their A.F.S. duties, 'except during an air raid when all four of us were on duty. After a while we received a uniform - trousers dark blue with a red stripe down each side and a tunic, gas mask and tin helmet.' By 1942 they had become 'full-fledged firemen' performing vital services. (Letter, 27 February 1995).

Jack Shepherd was an early volunteer, joining the A.F.S. in March 1938. When war was declared he tried to enlist with the Royal Warwicks. They refused him because he had glowing reports from both the Fire Brigade and his employers, Colmore Depot of Cherrywood Road, Bordesley Green. When the Blitz began, he was like tens of thousands of others 'working all day at their war jobs and then donning uniforms, armbands etc to work all night on whatever their allotted duties, specials, ARP, firewatch, Red Cross, St John's etc'. Jack's wife also worked and their son, John, was minded by his gran in Chichelly Street.

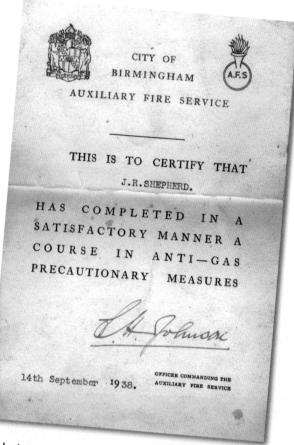

CITY OF BIRMINGHAM

A.F.S

AUXILIARY FIRE SERVICE

THIS IS TO CERTIFY THAT

J.R. SHEPHERD.

HAS COMPLETED IN A SATISFACTORY MANNER A COURSE IN ANTI—GAS PRECAUTIONARY MEASURES

14th September 1938.

OFFICER COMMANDING THE
AUXILIARY FIRE SERVICE

Probably the very circumstances that forced Jack and Dot to see little of each other or their son, saved their lives. Their Wright Road home was engulfed in the flames of a severe raid on Saltley and reduced to rubble while Dot was collecting the baby from Nan's in Vauxhall after munitions work. 'Mona the siren' sounded and she ran yet again to the communal air-raid shelter under the kids' play yard in Vauxhall Road. Jack was manning a pump escape on the goods yard 'pumping the canals into steam on the flames', as the bombers droned overhead and the incendiary bombs rained down on Brum. House gone, Jack for a while lived out of a locker at his Ralph Road fire station and a cardboard suitcase at work, Dot and young John were on the settee at Nan's. (John Shepherd, Letter, 20 August 1996).

The Ralph Road station, Saltley was wrecked by a bomb later in the war and Jack and his colleagues were moved to Ward End.

The operations of an A.F.S. fire station were described in February 1941 in the *Birmingham Post*. The control room was in a garage and on the walls were a calendar, lists and a map of the division. When the Home Guard or a warden called for help then a numbered pin was stuck in the street where the fire was raging. At all times one vehicle had to remain at the station. There was a book in which every telephone message was recorded and a long list of streets which detailed the nearest available water supply - whether from mains, canals, the River Rea, streams or storage tanks. This information was essential as only one engine carried water. Next door to the control room was a house where the men ate and slept. There were forty paid fire-fighters and 120 part-time volunteers - although the numbers available were always lower because of attendance on courses such as those concerning first aid and anti-gas measures. ('Auxiliary Fire Service', *Birmingham Post*, 20 February 1940).

The dangers faced by all fire-fighters impressed themselves on Mr F. Bayliss. He lived in a 'little house' in Leach Street, Ladywood.

When the war started I remember the enemy planes coming over the district and dropping their bombs every place where it mattered. The worst place I can recall was Docker's Paints where a few firemen were killed as they tackled the fires, as their boots were stuck to the hot paints and oils. Around then my father was a night watch warden at the Canning & Wildblood jam factory in Freeth Street. He used to come home and tell of all the places which had been hit in the night, then he would have breakfast and set off back to work. (Letter, April 1995).

A.F.S. personnel fighting a fire on the Moseley Road, Balsall Heath, 25 October 1940.

During the war the Fire Service dealt with 5,293 fire calls during 330 alerts which lasted a total of 663 hours. Seventeen men were killed on duty, and 23 were given honours. Amongst them were Auxiliary Fireman Robert Knight of Darwin Street who gained the George Medal for his courage when Brummie firefighters were sent to a fierce blaze at Pembroke Dock. Station Officer William Mosedale received Birmingham's first George Cross for his actions when an A.F.S. station at Grantham Road, Sparkbrook was destroyed by a high explosive bomb. William led the tunnelling and propping operations for the rescue of entombed men. Reaching the control room he found that there were other men he could not approach. Accordingly he carried out a digging operation from a different direction and saved four lives. Then he went to an adjoining house in which the cellar had collapsed. Persevering in his task he rescued four more people. Immediately he began tunnelling again to approach others who were in danger in the station's basement. Another four men were found alive. The cellar caved in shortly after the last person was removed. These operations. 'which lasted more than twelve hours, were carried out under intense bombardment'. (Harry Klopper, *The Fight Against Fire. The History of the Birmingham Fire and Ambulance Service*, Tunbridge Wells, 1954, p. 83; 'Stuck up a ladder as all around me burned', April 1941. *Evening Mail Special*, April 1981, p. 8; 'First Birmingham George Cross', *Birmingham Post*, 29 March 1941).

There were a number of private fire brigades run by factories, including an all female troop at the Boxfoldia Works in Selly Oak, and throughout Birmingham trained fire-fighters were helped by groups of Brummies who formed sector fire parties. Supplied with buckets of sand, scoops and stirrup pumps, their members were instructed at their nearest fire station and until late 1940 they were attached to the Air Raid

Wardens' Service. After that time they became part of an independent unit gathered in divisions, although they continued to share the accommodation of wardens and had corresponding ranks. The Highgate and Sparkbrook Division of the Fire Guards' Service was based at a large house on the Moseley Road and it was headed by Wes Barrett. He was a partner in an engineering business in Angelina Street, Highgate and had a keen interest in his local fire party. They realised the inadequacies of stirrup pumps in fighting fires and together they devised a mobile fire engine. Mr Narborough was Deputy Assistant Chief Fire Guard Officer for the Moseley area and recalled that Mr Barrett's idea was not unique as many other parties had the same idea. Still 'the Angelina Street turnout was considered the best. Essentially, the device was a 40 gallon steel drum mounted on a wheel chassis and with an efficient hand pump and a long hose'. As the war drew to a close, the engine and its operators were drawn and the picture was displayed in the Art Gallery. (Letter, 1984).

Fire-watching was a crucial task in the prevention of major blazes. From October 1940 it was compulsory for factories and works to employ trained night-watchmen, and early the next year this scheme was extended. Everyone aged between 16 and 60 became liable for part-time work in the Civil Defence Forces. In particular, men were compelled to serve as fire watchers for 48 hours each month, with the instruction that 'protection of their workplaces will take precedence over protection of their homes'. ('Fire Watch Plan', *Birmingham Mail*, 18 January 1941). Ray Cooper's mom and dad managed Hamilton's butcher's shop on High Street, Aston. Their flat was above the shop and 'during the war our living room was the local fire-watchers headquarters'. On the wall there was a board 'with the keys of all the shops from Aston Brook Street to Burlington Street' and 'the managers from the shops took it in turns to be on duty each night during the blitz'. (Letter, 28 July 1996).

A training session for auxiliary firemen at Holloway Head, 27 October 1940.

Such firewatchers contributed greatly to diminishing the effects of burnings caused by enemy bombing. One of their number was Len Baron of Highgate. He worked for J.S. Wright, a firm of plumbers at 85½ Dale End. At about 6.00 p.m. on the night of 9 April 1941 he and two colleagues began to look out for fire, hoping to have a quiet night free from bombing.

But alas this was not to be, because at about 8 PM the air raid warning siren sounded followed by the well known 'hum drum' of the German bombers. So we had to prepare ourselves for action. Because the bombs began to fall around the city centre accompanied by the assuring rat-tat of our anti aircraft fire. At about 11 PM we discovered that our water supply had failed so we engineered an idea of draining down the water out of the central heating system. It came in very useful for the stirrup pumps with which to douche the incendiary bombs which had fallen upon our property. As I remember we had a very hectic night which finally came to end when the 'all clear' sounded at about 3 AM. But somehow we knew that the centre of Birmingham had been hit very hard. After some further consultation I was given permission to be allowed to go home. I remember walking through lengths of hose pipes which had become useless owing to lack of water. During my walk home I was reminded by air-raid wardens and auxiliary firemen shouting and warning me 'don't go down there mate there's an unexploded bomb' or 'don't walk too near that building it's liable to collapse'.

Approaching his home in Conybere Street, Len saw to his horror that in Gooch Street 'The Bridge' pub had been obliterated with a direct hit. Seventeen people had taken shelter in its cellar. All were killed. Depressed, he was met on his door step by his 63 year old mom and all she said was 'hasn't it been a night'. It was six in the morning. Len had something to eat, a good wash and without any rest for a day he wearily went to work. The next night he was exhausted and fell asleep. He was awoken by water trickling through the ceiling in half a dozen places. The land mine which had destroyed 'The Bridge' had displaced slates on the roof of his house and rainfall 'simply petered through'. Calmly and matter-of-factly he and his mom placed buckets and bowls under the leaks to catch the water: 'We didn't mind this inconvenience for we were more than grateful that we were still alive'. (Letter, 31 March 1995).

Fire watchers were not always workers, some of them were owners of businesses. Brooke Adie was a director of his family firm in the Jewellery Quarter. During one raid he 'remained on the roof for over an hour in dangerous conditions, and only left when the roof started to collapse'. Reaching the outside of the burning building, Brooke became aware that the '11,000 volts high tension electric supply and transformers were alive, and endangering the lives of the contingent of the city fire brigade'. He rushed back inside and shut off the power supply 'at great personal risk'. The rest of the night he spent fighting the fire. For his courage and leadership he was awarded the British Empire Medal. ('Raid Bravery', *Birmingham Mail*, 17 May 1941).

The lives of Dianne Wedgebury and her mom were saved by the actions of fire-watchers and air raid wardens. Her family lived on the Coventry Road by Elmdon 'but in 1941 we moved to Edgbaston, as my mother (a former nurse) wanted to help the war effort. She was offered a job at the Red Cross in Highfield Road, Edgbaston & they offered us the large house next door.' Beneath it was a large cellar which was used as a shelter. One night it took a direct hit and Dianne 'can remember screaming as the house shook and fell'. Fortunately the basement held and mother and daughter were dug out of the rubble by A.R.P. people. Dianne was taken to a first-aid unit, 'but I had no serious injuries, only some hearing loss' and her mother was unhurt. Her dad was outside helping the fire-watchers when the bomb exploded and 'he was blown from one side of the road to the other by the blast - but only suffered minor injuries'. Sadly there were fatalities and 'the young bobby-on-the-beat was one of those killed - he was found under the brickwork that had been the front of our house'. (Letter, 11 April 1995).

Saving Lives: Medical Services

A.R.P. volunteers, 23 April 1940.

Like Dianne's mother, members of the Red Cross and the St John's Ambulance Brigade were crucial in the ambulance service and by the end of October 1939 their numbers had swollen to almost 5,000 volunteers. Doreen Vaughan was another of them. Based at the Northfield Centre, every night she and other volunteers went 'all over Birmingham to deal with people bombed out of their houses and places of work. Her daughter recalls 'she saw some dreadful sights enough to make anyone's hair stand on end'. (Marilyn Vaughan, Letter, 27 March 1995). Often the vehicles used by Doreen and her comrades were improvised business vans and motor cars, although from November 1939 new ambulances were brought into use. These had room for four stretcher cases and were mounted on the chassis of private cars. The Birmingham Hospital Saturday Fund was active in providing ambulances, paying for five by early September 1940. ('Fifth Ambulance', *Birmingham Mail*, 3 September 1940).

Connected to these ambulance personnel were those belonging to Rescue Parties which were set up in 1939. There were 120 Light Rescue Parties of seven men each, and 30 Heavy Rescue Parties made up of eighteen men split in two shifts. Each party was headed by a foreman, like Horace Edward Jones of Runcorn Road, Balsall Heath. He gained a British Empire Medal for his valour in one air raid. The front of a house had fallen down and Horace saved three children and two adults. Another man was pinned down, having a broken leg. Horace freed him and set the limb in splints. He and his men then 'worked through the night and the remaining two adults were extricated'. On another occasion he was joined by two other rescue foremen from Balsall Heath, Arthur Hudson of Lincoln Street and Robert Porter of Jakeman

Road. They 'made gallant attempts to rescue five people trapped in a cellar'. Tragically their striving was to no avail. The cellar walls and ceiling collapsed, killing the five Brummies. ('Bravery in Raids', *Birmingham Mail*, 14 June 1941).

The First Aid Service was also established in 1939. It had 3,400 members organised in 340 parties, each of which was divided into two shifts. To supplement the services of hospitals, thirty-two first-aid posts were established. Most were in public baths and schools. The aim was that no-one with minor injuries would be more than a mile from a post where there were qualified nurses and auxiliaries such as Rhoda Evans, then Gunn. Living in Gooch Street, Highgate she had registered for nursing duties before the outbreak of war. On 1 September 1939 she and her friend, Joan Ward, were told to report in uniform at Moor Street Station and help with evacuation procedures. They joined Dr Louis Glass, a dozen or so orderlies of the St John's Ambulance Brigade, 'about six sisters (two had been to Siberia in the First World War and one had been to the front in France) and a dozen assorted females aged between 18 and 56 each of whom had a minimum basic training of ninety hours'. After helping at the station Rhoda and Joan were 'assigned to No. 7 Ambulance Train based at Monument Lane Station'. Their main task was to accompany sick people to 'areas that were considered to be of greater safety'. One 'terrible night' in Birmingham she, her dad and others took an injured person to the First-Aid Post at Kent Street Baths:

St John's Ambulance Brigade volunteers from Oscott Division. Superintendent Charles Edward Casson is sitting to the left of the trophy. A toolmaker from Kingstanding, during the war he was out most nights and weekends on first-aid duty.

> *What a sight greeted us when we got there. A bomb had just fallen, a direct hit, and chaos reigned. The duty sister was in a daze and only wanted a cup of tea, but all I could get was a bottle of milk. On the stairs lay two young girls who had been stripped naked by the blast. Their bones were sticking through their skin. The people on duty would not let us downstairs even though I was in my nurse's uniform and the others were first-aiders. My father and George Morgan fetched blankets to cover the girls and George said that he never thought that he would live to see a woman's modesty exposed in that manner for all to see. It sounds old-fashioned now but it was the sentiment of a more honourable generation.*

Rhoda heard a little sound and saw a slight movement. In the rubble lay a nurse who was bleeding. Rhoda bathed the injured woman's face with water from a bucket and tried to stop the blood going into her eyes and mouth, recalling 'I had never really smelt blood before'. (Letter, 1995)

The Women's Voluntary Service were prominent at First-Aid Posts. One of their members was Peggy Williams of the Chester Road, Erdington. She worked as a secretary at Birlec in Tyburn Road, helped with the National Savings Scheme and 'out of working hours I went on duty at a First Aid Post, which I believe was at Erdington Swimming Baths, and dispensed tea and sympathy from a W.V.S. tea urn - little realising that I would later spend 40 years with that worthy organisation'. (Letter, April 1995). The Women's Voluntary Services for Civil Defence had been organised a year before the war and by the end of the conflict had 20,400 members in Birmingham. They were an unpaid, non-uniformed 'army of women who gave up leisure, comfort and sleep to minister to the needs of anyone who called upon their services'. Their contribution to the war effort was great and varied. They darned socks for servicemen; they cleaned military hospitals; they cooked meals for air-raid victims 'on emergency stoves made from bricks gathered from the wreckage'; they helped at control centres; they provided canteen facilities for the Home Guard and for wounded soldiers at railway stations; they sat up with invalids and expectant mothers during the Blitz; and they recovered the belongings of those made homeless by bombing. Their efforts were matched by the volunteers of the Lord Mayor of Birmingham's War Relief Fund 'which gave aid and comfort to tens of thousands of people'. ('Women's Magnificent Voluntary Service', *Birmingham Post Supplement*, 8 May 1945; Harold J. Black, *History of the Corporation of Birmingham, Volume VI. 1936-1950. Part I*, Birmingham, 1957, p. 87).

There were twelve mobile first-aid units based at six stations. They went to major incidents and coped with heavy casualties before they were taken to hospital. As D. Jones emphasised, the vital work of doctors and nurses continued following the Blitz when badly injured troops were treated with 'care and devotion' in places such as the Queen Elizabeth Hospital. (Letter, April 1995). After the General Hospital was bombed late in 1940, two emergency basement facilities were established. One was at Lewis' Department Store in Corporation Street and the other was at the Aston Cross Brewery of Ansells. Both companies installed sinks, lights, screens and other equipment, whilst the government provided beds, stretchers and other

An A.R.P. first-aid training session on the Dudley Road, Winson Green, 19 September 1939.

furniture. Each 'shadow hospital' also had X-Ray apparatus and an operating theatre and could cope with 100 casualties at a time. ('Emergency Hospital at Birmingham Shop', *Birmingham Post*, 27 February 1941).

During the worst air raids on Birmingham many of the injured were sent to hospitals outside the city. Mrs I. A. Fenton was a Hungarian who had come to Britain to learn English and then had joined the 'Civil Nursing Reserve in Bromsgrove as a Nursing Auxiliary'. She served at Barnsley Hall War Emergency Hospital where 'we had all sorts of patients - besides the forces - civilians, women, children, old people, bombed out of Birmingham'. (Letter, 17 April 1995). Victims of the Blitz were not the only ones treated at facilities such as this. Doreen Harris M.B.E. 'was in Dudley Road hospital with ulcerative colitis, for which later I had an ileostomy'. One day without any notice 'I was put into an ambulance and taken (very ill indeed) to Burntwood psychiatric hospital near Lichfield'. She and other patients were put in huts which 'had been built in the grounds to take wounded soldiers if the need occurred'. They were treated 'very well'. (Letter, 24 April 1996).

A gas mask drill for nurses at the General Hospital, Whittal Street side, 5 September 1939.

Initially those folk who were uninjured but homeless were cared for by volunteers in a rest centre supplied with clothes and food. By August 1941 the A.R.P. Committee had set up 100 of these facilities, many of which were provided by the churches. From rest centres the homeless were sent to one of 50 hostels. Run by stewards and stewardesses they could cope with up to 2,500 people, whilst another 50,000 folk could be billeted 'in ordinary residences where occupants are in a position to take in bombed-out people'. Another feature of A.R.P. was the provision of 130 Emergency Feeding Centres where 120,000 Brummies could be given food paid for by the city. Most were in schools with reserve water tanks and solid fuel boilers, in case the supplies of gas and electricity were cut off. ('After-Raid Care', Birmingham Mail, 1 August 1940).

Awful Jobs: Police Officers

In the preparations for war a crucial role was assigned to the police. Officers were influential not only in maintaining public order but also in A.R.P. work. From 1938 they were instructed to assist the Air Raid Warden's Service and to act as anti-gas instructors. In particular the police were responsible for protecting munitions factories and in enforcing the blackout. As a young child in Hall Green, Brian Henderson was unaware of the difficulties faced by his own policeman dad. In common with other officers he worked tiring eight hour shifts in rotation, with the first watch beginning at 6.00 a.m. In retrospect his son realised that his dad and all policemen 'had some

Winston Churchill, Prime Minister of the United Kingdom, at the badly-bombed Holloway Head, inspecting Birmingham policemen who won awards for gallantry, 26 September 1941. P.C. Ronald Jackson, George Medallist, is second from the right.

awful jobs to do in wartime Birmingham. Quite often they were first on the scene when bombs fell locally. They then had to deal with their own feelings besides having to help others, including gathering up various remains.' (Letter, 25 March, 1996).

The courage of policemen is indicated by the awards for gallantry and operational efficiency given to 35 of them. Amongst them were three George Medallists. One was received by Constable Thomas Henwood for the 'outstanding bravery and initiative' he showed when he organised fire watchers in a chain to pass on water and so prevented a serious blaze. In another attack he dug through debris to save a man and a woman who were trapped and injured. Because of the 'dangerous conditions of the building' he would not let anyone assist him. Another act of bravery was carried out by Sergeant Charles Ward. A bomb failed to go off at Webley and Scott's, the gunmakers of Weaman Street. Charles found that the top of the explosive was loose. He put his hand in, scooping out the explosive like soft cheese to reach the fuse from inside'. Then he placed the mechanism in a bucket of water. Charles was awarded the British Empire Medal, as was Special Constable Emmanuel Graham. Throughout the attacks on Birmingham he showed courage and determination, conveying police and rescuers to places where they were needed and helping in a number of rescues. ('Further Awards for Raid Gallantry', *Birmingham Weekly Post*, 27 June 1941; Arthur Steele, 'UXB - the Midland Heroes', *Evening Mail*, 5 March 1979).

The regular police force was aided greatly not only by specials but also by a Women's Auxiliary Police Corps whose members performed clerical and driving duties. Further assistance was given by members of the Police Auxiliary Messenger Service. They were aged between sixteen and eighteen and kept communications open between Birmingham's police stations. One of their number was Mr R.P. Meredith, who was stationed at Harborne. He went about on a bicycle, trying to avoid not only bomb explosions but also 'crumbling buildings with flying masonry and glass everywhere' as well as 'red hot jagged pieces of shrapnel falling to earth from our own anti-aircraft shells'. All the messengers travelled through streets which:

> were littered with debris and bomb craters with fire hoses snaking everywhere across their path, past blazing fires - toppling buildings, past blazing gas mains and ruptured water mains flooding the roads already congested with Civil Defence vehicles and stranded cars, and always with the pungent smell of coal gas escaping from broken pipes. Frequently detours had to be made where roads and streets were cordoned off because of unexploded bombs, or land mines caught up in parachutes hanging from trees, denied an impact which would have erased whole streets, flattening them completely, and that was a frequent occurrence. (Letter, 22 February 1995).

Beneath Ground: the Provision of Shelters

Corporation workers had a significant impact in preparing Brum to withstand air raids. The City's Estates Department was involved in rehousing families whose houses were blitzed and in repairing bomb-damaged dwellings, whilst the Public Works Department (P.W.D.) recruited and trained Decontamination, Rescue and Repair Parties. The P.W.D. was also responsible for most of the building work which was carried out for the A.R.P. services; it provided equipment; and it erected and designated shelters. During August 1938, in the more densely-populated neighbourhoods of Birmingham, basements were surveyed and classified. In the next month the P.W.D. prepared, marked and strengthened a number of these sites. Over the same period, trench shelters were dug in parks and open ground. Mostly they could take 50 people and they were reinforced with steel, concrete and linings. During the phoney war, brick-built surface shelters were erected at schools like Colmore Road in Kings Heath, cellars beneath houses were made stronger, and a number of public shelters were constructed for those Brummies who were unable to reach home when an air-raid warning was sounded.

These measures were in addition to the tens of thousands of Anderson steel surface shelters which were distributed from February 1939. Designed to withstand the effects of a 500lb hitting the ground 20 feet distant, most Anderson Shelters were free - although better-off folk were expected to pay for them. Jean Perks' dad was amongst the first to take one, erecting it in their back garden in Winson Green. His efforts were decried by a neighbour who 'mockingly called out, "What a waste of time, you'll never need that." How wrong she was!' This particular shelter was well-equipped with wooden floor, bunks, light and food. (Letter, 21 February 1995). By 15 November 1939 the *Birmingham Mail* reported that the city's 100,000th Anderson Shelter had been delivered to Mr Kain of 210 Musgrave Road, Winson Green. Like all of them, it had come from factories in South Wales and had been transported in a major operation by the Great Western and the London, Midland and Scottish Railways. ('100,000 Shelters', *Birmingham Mail*, 15 November 1939).

Each shelter weighed between two and three hundredweight and had to be put in a hole four feet deep. To make room for their 'Anderson', Ruby Trigg's husband had to dig up their lilac trees and bed of flowers in their small garden in Handsworth. Because the shelter was 'bitterly cold' during the winter months', the couple devised a means of heating it. Each morning they lit a candle in a large clay pot and placed a similar pot over it. By the evening the shelter was 'quite warm'. The couple also had two chairs to sleep in and a cot for their baby - although they could not permanently leave pillows and blankets in the shelter because of the dampness. (Letter, 17 September 1996). This was a major problem, as was waterlogging in those parts of Birmingham through which ran streams and brooks. Margaret Smith was one of many Brummies who had to abandon her Anderson Shelter. Living in Watery Lane, Bordesley, she 'used to try and grow flowers in the soil covering it because we hadn't got a garden'. (Letter, 23 June 1996). Violet Hoare of Nechells experienced similar problems:

> I remember the Anderson shelter sunk into our garden, its corrugated iron dome covered in earth and sandbags and inside the dank, damp atmosphere that prevailed and encouraged all kinds of insects to take up residence in there, I was frightened to sleep in case some inquisitive earwig decided to explore inside my ear. My mother was far from happy with this 'bolt hole' so she decided we would be just as safe on the brick-built cellar head facing the cellar steps under the stairs inside the house; so, on a mattress, there we would lie like sardines in a tin, mom, my young sister and me. Even there we had an unwelcome visitor. I recall my mother waking up thinking that my sister was tapping her face only to realise that a mouse was taking a constitutional across her face, she picked him up by his tail and threw him down the cellar steps and there he was running round in circles completely disorientated. My father was in the part time fire service . . . (Letter, 17 February 1995).

Not all Anderson Shelters were useless. On the night of 22-23 November a bomb hit the shop belonging to Charlie Crowe's mom in Hallam Street, Balsall Heath: 'the shelter undoubtedly saved our lives, but my mother lost her living, her home and lots of possessions as I did myself'. (Letter, 17 July 1996).

Most Anderson Shelters were situated in the suburbs and in places where houses had back gardens. There were fewer of them in the older central neighbourhoods of Birmingham where space was more limited and where reliance was put on reinforced house cellars. Many back-to-backs were not provided with this form of protection, and from February 1941

Ann and Sheila Williams in their front garden at Chatwell Grove, Weoley Castle. Behind them is their family's Anderson Shelter, covered with earth and its entrance sandbagged.

Morrison Shelters were handed out. These were steel tables, 6' 6" long and 4' wide, each with a steel mesh side for entrance and a sprung floor to allow a mattress to be placed within. They were set up inside houses and were reckoned to be able to resist the crashing of a dwelling. As an eight-year old, Richard Lewis lived in Upper Highgate Street. With other members of St Albans Scout Troop, 'the Sprouts as we were known', he helped his seniors to erect these table shelters 'for the elderly, earning ourselves a National Service Badge, which we proudly wore on our uniform'. His own family's Morrison Shelter filled most of the living room, but 'I found it ideal for doing jigsaw puzzles and running my trains on'. Richard spent many nights 'caged', listening to the sound of the bombs, especially the whistling ones, as they seemed to make their way down the street, then waiting for the bang, the shaking & the rumbling of the falling buildings that followed & the question being asked "I wonder who has caught that one?! - it sounded close"'. There was one noise which was not frightening and which gave him and others some comfort. This was the boom of 'Big Bertha' - 'the anti-aircraft gun in Highgate Park, which gave us the feeling that at least we were hitting back at the enemy'. (Letter, 27 February 1995).

Mrs Stevens in the entrance to her family's shelter in their back garden at 22, Branksome Avenue, Handsworth. Her husband had surrounded the shelter with concrete and on the roof he was making a fish pond with a miniature waterfall, 25 September 1939.

As the war went on, the authorities erected small, brick shelters in many yards of back-to-backs. Emily Louise Robinson and her husband, Joe, 'had no faith in these fragile structures but we thought it was better than having the whole house collapse on us, so we decided to make use of it'. Joe built bunk beds for the shelter and filled a bucket with fuel so that they could light a fire and keep warm. The shelter saved their lives. One night explosions and gunfire blasted away the silence. Then there was a 'terrific' bang 'followed by the sound of soil and stones raining down; we thought it would never cease'. The adults forced a way through the rubble and when they came out they saw that three large houses and a shop 'had been completely flattened'. The shopkeeper and one of his daughters were dead. His wife and other children had sheltered on the cellar steps and were rescued from the ruins. Five other people from the terrace were killed, including a fifteen-year old fire-watcher and a person who was 'burned so badly his body had been reduced to the size of a child'. (Emily Louise Robinson, *Must This Happen Again?*, unpublished manuscript, 1982, pp. 5-6).

Some families had to resort to public shelters or those provided by local factories. Many families used the facilities of Docker's, the varnish makers in Rotton Park Street, Ladywood. One night P.B.M.'s family should have gone there 'but owing to myself being ill, with the usual chest complaint and the weather was bitterly cold, mother decided to keep us in our usual spot on the stairs to take our chances. Another of God's blessings. That factory took a direct hit and most people were killed.' (Letter, 20 February 1995). Although her family did have an Anderson Shelter, Betty Smith, then Bicknell, did not like it 'as no-one could lie down on the bunks my dad had made'. Supplied with a flask, sandwiches and a blanket she preferred the facilities at Hughes's Biscuit Factory in Bordesley Green Road.

> One night it was very noisy and my dad came to take me home. He had a job to get in the shelter, as it was packed and he just couldn't get past the wardens. I can still see his face when he found me. He said, 'Come on home, your Mom wants you'. Well I had a shock when we got out of the shelter. Everywhere seemed to be burning. We came out of the shelter at the far end, we went over the ground we used to call the tip, and was making our way to come along a driveway at the side of the recreation ground. But it was like daylight from all the fires. I actually saw a plane machine gunning the people below. We had to dive in the ditch a couple of times as the planes came over. We came to the bottom of our entry. I left my dad putting out incendiary bombs. Never the less I was terrified and was I glad to be back in our own shelter. (Letter, 5 March 1995).

Jean Smith, then Lewis, came out of Bishopsgate Street and with her mom and dad sought protection beneath the premises of Hangar Motors in Broad Street. To her child's eyes the shelter 'seemed to be filled with hundreds of bunks which you could sleep on during the raids'. It was here that she met her 'first Asian family', who 'always sat behind the sandbags close to the entrance in Tennant Street'. Sadly, these people were suffocated one night when the sandbags fell upon them. (Letter, 14 February 1996). Most workplaces appointed employees to take charge of such shelters. These volunteers were helped by other workers, amongst them Frances Winstanley of the GEC, Witton. She looked after medical equipment - 'dressings, bandages, water, sal-volatile etc, as much as a strong man could manage to carry, let alone a seven stone stripling like me'. (Winstanley, *Sparrers Can't Sing*, p. 155).

Despite the great number of shelters, there were numerous people who had to rely on their own ingenuity for protection. Olive Brown's parents, the Sidwells, had a greengrocer's in Camden Street, Brookfields. Her dad, Walter, 'reinforced our cellar and made it into a veritable fortress. He even built an emergency exit to the yard'. During the war 'two landmines fell simultaneously'. Aiming for Hockley Goods Station across the road, one fell in Tenby Street and the other demolished Ellen Street School. As they exploded, Walter was going upstairs in his home and he 'was blown from top to bottom of the stairs, shaken but unhurt'. (Letter, 15 March 1996). The effects of the explosion on the shelter at the school were described by Alice, who was in the Civil Nursing Reserve:

> Well there were lots of people in there and when we got there relatives were all hysterical, screaming and trying to get into the rubble and we had to get the police to clear them out so that the rescue men could work. And we'd go in with the rescue men. If we saw a limb we'd feel to see if there was any sign of life - if there was,

well the rescue men would work on them and we'd be giving injections of morphia and we had blue pencils which we used to write either on the arm, the head or the leg how much morphia and what time it was given. That was a very bad shell there. There were lots and lots of dead there, I'm afraid. (Birmingham City Council, Department of Leisure and Community Services, Museums and Arts Division, *Waiting for the All Clear. Life in Birmingham During the Second World War*, Birmingham, 1995).

Striking Back: Anti-Aircraft

Searchlight practice, 6 August 1939.

The precautions against air raids were varied. Mrs I. Madkins lived in Bennetts Road, Saltley. Each 'evening at around dusk a group of soldiers believed to be the pioneer corps marched down the roads around this area, and poured into huge smoking cans (which were placed at regular intervals on both sides of the road) old used engine oil'. This was lit 'and sent into the atmosphere thick black smoke which was designed to conceal the railway marshalling yards and the gas holders and numerous munitions factories nearby'. (Letter, 22 May 1995). Floating above the smog were cigar-shaped barrage balloons, attached to the ground with steel cables. Their purpose was to make enemy bombers fly higher, lessening their accuracy and making them easier targets for the searchlights and fire from light and heavy anti-aircraft units.

Denis S. Green was a member of an AA battery, '378 Company of the 45th. (Searchlight) Battalion Royal Engineers'. Formed shortly before the war as a Territorial Army unit it was attached to the Royal Warwickshire Regiment, but on 1 August 1940 it was transferred to the Royal Regiment of Artillery. The company was deployed close to Coleshill 'with Lewis Guns of the First World War vintage, mounted on ex-railway sleepers in the anti-aircraft defence of Hams Hall power station'. Its members maintained that their unit was the first to open fire in the Second World War. Late on the afternoon of 3 September 1939 'an unmarked plane flew over the area and one of our detachments' shot at it. It was rumoured that the pilot was French and that he landed with a wound at Castle Bromwich aerodrome. (Peter Leather, 'Hidden City', *Metronews*, 30 May 1996).

Ack-ack units were sited in Birmingham's parks and large open spaces - themselves mostly situated around the central neighbourhoods of the city. One of them was placed in Hobmoor Road, on the edge of Small Heath. As Norma Westwick remembered, it was attacked by the German bombers. First they dropped flares - 'numerous balls of light, which suspended in the air, for them to see more clearly where their targets were'.

> *We had one set of flares over the back door and another over our air raid shelter. I remember the anguish of my parents not knowing whether to stay in the house or make a run for the shelter for fear of being machine gunned, they decided on the latter and we all made a run for it. We could hear the orders of the Ack-Ack commander quite clearly, number one gun, get ready, fire, number two gun, get ready fire and so on. The next air raid we were waiting for those famous words but sadly they never came. We heard there had been a direct hit and it had put the lot out of action, killing the commander and his men.* (Letter, 14 June 1995).

Brenda Bullock has almost the same memory. She lived a few miles from an anti-aircraft battery in Sheldon, 'yet in the quiet between the whistle and bang of the bombs dropping and the explosions made by the guns firing, we could distinctly hear the officer in charge of the guns shouting his orders for his men to fire'. Over many months 'his voice had offered us a comforting familiarity and reassurance as we huddled in the shelter'. In particular, the adults felt that 'we were at least giving Jerry a taste of his own medicine' and it gave them 'some bleak satisfaction in thinking that we weren't just victims: we could fight back'. One night as Brenda dozed fitfully she was awoken by an enormous explosion. Everyone gathered 'their scattered wits' and suddenly 'we became aware of the silence - no more shouted orders from the gun battery'. It dawned upon them that the unit had taken a direct hit. Brenda looked around in the gloom and was astonished to see that all the family 'had tears running unchecked down their cheeks'. As she became

Anti-aircraft battery, 5 July 1942.

older she understood their grief. That night 'they had lost a friend, a disembodied voice that symbolised their resistance to what was happening to them, an ally who struck back at the enemy for them while they remained impotently in their shelter'. (Brenda Bullock, *A Pocket With A Hole. A Birmingham Childhood of the 1940s and 1950s*, Studley, 1996, p.18).

Upsets and Disappointments: Concerns over A.R.P.

For all the activity of the A.R.P. Committee and for all the efforts of tens of thousands of people, there were difficulties with Birmingham's preparations for Civil Defence. According to Harry Klopper, the A.F.S. was 'not quite ready' when war was declared. For a few days afterwards 'chaos reigned: Anderson shelters were rushed to stations, both regular and A.F.S; and sandbagging went on everywhere'. As in other places the lack of funds was the biggest stumbling block and officers 'had to dig into their own pockets to provide money for their men who had not received any pay or had to buy food while away from home for long periods'. The A.F.S. was not alone, all A.R.P. services were affected by similar problems. In this confused situation 'the ten months of the "phoney" war were a godsend'. (Klopper, *The Fight Against Fire*, p. 81).

Klopper was right. The respite in the war did provide time for the authorities to speed up civil defence preparations, but also it encouraged complacency. The number of A.R.P. workers dropped drastically by some 15,000 to about 40,000 by 18 June 1940. It was revealed that more A.F.S. personnel and despatch riders were required, that rescue squads and stretcher bearers were at half strength, that wardens were short in some localities, and that thousands of women first-aid volunteers had gone missing. So great was the need for A.R.P. workers that councillors set up soap boxes on street corners to 'explain the needs of the moment'. Within a short time, volunteers had responded to the calls for recruitment - activated by the graveness of the situation on the continent where France had fallen to the Nazis. ('Ambulance Drivers Needed', *Birmingham Mail*, 18 June 1940).

Men of the '24' age group registering for military service at the Birmingham Central Employment Exchange, 9 March 1940.

There were concerns in other fields. During the Blitz there was a widespread feeling that the government was not giving Birmingham enough financial support. These misgivings and resentments were stressed in a *Birmingham Mail* editorial headlined 'City's War Burden' on 22 May 1941.

What the harassed ratepayer wants is a speedy decision by the Government that what is undoubtedly a part of the national war effort should be included in the calls on the Treasury and not on the rates. Birmingham is one of the localities in the forefront of the Battle of Britain, and its defence is as essential to the taxpayer in a safe area as to the local ratepayer.

The Government was also noticeable for its lack of financial support in other areas. There was a great worry that a direct hit on a public shelter might lead to massive casualties, and in 1941 a demand grew for constructing deep and bomb-proof shelters. None were built because of the great cost involved and because it was felt that the soil of Birmingham was not conducive to such structures. ('Raid Shelters in Birmingham', *Birmingham Post*, 2 May 1941).

In general, the whole subject of shelters proved contentious. On 3 January 1941, the A.R.P. Committee stated that the provision of shelters continued 'to present a problem of immense magnitude'. Over 31,000 Anderson Shelters were waterlogged, many others had been damaged in air raids, and there were insufficient men and materials to carry out repairs. Accordingly, it was decided that no more public shelters should be built and that attention should focus on domestic shelters. A programme was announced of providing surface shelters, erecting Anderson shelters inside homes in those areas where there had been flooding, and of strengthening basements. ('Public Shelters', *Birmingham Mail*, 3 January 1941)

Just over a week later a journalist was sent out to find why 'do hundreds of Birmingham people go every night, fair weather or foul, raid or no raid, to sleep in the city's public shelters'. It appeared that bomb damage had made many homes almost uninhabitable, large numbers of shelters were unusable because of wetness, and some cellars had not been reinforced. The investigator also revealed the inadequacy of trench shelters. That in Macdonald Street was solidly constructed and free from flooding - 'but not from the damp caused by condensation'. Bedding was sodden, lighting was primitive and narrow benches were the only furniture. ('Shelter Night Life in Birmingham', *Birmingham Post*, 11 February 1941). These revelations contradicted the claim made by Councillor Tiptaft that there was no need for any Brummie 'to sleep in public shelters because of the alleged lack of other accommodation', and they indicated that there were problems with A.R.P. throughout the Blitz on Birmingham.

Away from Home: Evacuation

There is little doubt that the Government was slow in beginning the provision of shelters in Birmingham. Its tardiness was caused by two factors: first by the belief that in the event of war aerial bombing would be concentrated on London; and second by the assumption that the main defence against attacks by planes would be the dispersal of the population. Accordingly, organised evacuation was a major feature of planning for war. From the mid-1930s instructions were sent to major local authorities, and in Birmingham's case the council had to assess the risks of bombing on different parts of the city. Following the Munich Crisis the Chief Education Officer was appointed as the city's Evacuation Officer and the city was divided into three zones. The central wards and those containing munitions works or public utilities were

Schoolchildren awaiting evacuation from Snow Hill Station, 8 September 1939.

regarded as 'Evacuation Areas'; in the inner ring as a whole, residential or partly residential districts were designated 'Neutral'; whilst residential suburbs were classed as 'Reception Areas'. Locally these distinctions were seen as 'somewhat meaningless' because of the immense war potential of the city as a whole. As Harold J. Black explained 'it seemed obvious enough that no bombing plan devised on a military basis by an unscrupulous enemy could possibly correspond with the arbitrary map-makings of a newly-fledged Civil Defence concept'. Constant pressure from the Corporation eventually led to the recognition of the whole of Birmingham as an Evacuation Area in 1941. [Black, *History of the Corporation of Birmingham*, p. 57].

Birmingham's scheme was based on an orderly evacuation taking place over two days. On the first day children would leave the city with their teachers. Each school was classified into primary, secondary, elementary, special and nursery, whilst private schools were to fit in where they could. The second day of evacuation was scheduled for expectant mothers and those with young children and for adults who were blind or disabled. Responsibility for these people was shared between Maternity and Child Welfare organisations and the After-Care departments of the Royal Institution for the Blind and what was then known as the Royal Cripples Hospital (now the Woodlands). On 20 July 1939 a test evacuation was carried out at Hockley railway station. It included nine schools, one of which was Burberry Street, Hockley where Ron Smith was a pupil. He arrived at the school at the normal time and waited for the bell to sound, signalling the children to line up in their classes. As they stood in the playground, their teachers went round checking that each child had 'clothes, footwear, toiletries, personal items, not forgetting of course our gas masks and identity cards'. Ron was approached by his teacher:

'Well Smith, where's your luggage?' 'Ere it is, sir, in 'ere', I replied. 'Is that all you have got lad, you won't be able to go far on that will you?' 'Our Mom sez we ain't guin anyw'ere, any road up, we've gorra stop at 'um with 'er an' dad, an' we've gorra stop tergetha, all onus.' He looked at me for a few seconds, with what I now realise as despair in his eyes, utter despair and utter sympathy. 'Well let's have a look at what you have got, although it won't be a lot will it, because of your gas mask being in there as well.' 'Mom don' believe in gas masks sir, she sez they ain't nachrul, an' she wunt lerus 'ave 'em.' 'Oh I see', more looks of despair and then he started to write furiously in his book. (Ron Smith, *A Paddle Down Hockley Brook*, Brierley Hill, no date, pp. 158-9).

With the prospect of war imminent, Emily Louise Robinson recalled that she and other mothers were called to their children's school in east Birmingham. It was filled to capacity with anxious looking women, some of them with toddlers and babies in arms. They listened intently to a speaker who told them that they were 'in a number one target area', surrounded by gas works, main railways and factories. He called upon them to take their children into the countryside', emphasising that 'we shall be facing a most unscrupulous and indomitable enemy'. The mothers were ordered take their gas masks with them on all occasions, and they were told about the different kinds of gases which the enemy might use. By the end of his lecture 'most of the women had made up their minds and it was now up to them to get the consent of their husbands to take their children to safety'. Emily and her three children were evacuated, but like many people they returned to Birmingham before the Blitz began. (Robinson, *'Must This Happen Again'*, pp. 1-3).

Adhering to government instructions, the city council decided that children were to be evacuated from those localities which were most at risk of enemy attack, roughly those within the Inner Circle 8 bus route. Close to the city centre they included Digbeth, Deritend, Bordesley, Gosta Green, Holloway Head, Summer Lane and the Gun Quarter. To the west they covered Spring Hill, Brookfields, Ladywood, Winson Green, Hockley, Soho, Gib Heath, much of Rotton Park and Handsworth, and a small section of Edgbaston. On the north they took in Aston, Birchfield, Lozells and a large part of Witton. To the east they embraced Nechells, Duddeston, Ashted, Vauxhall, Washwood Heath, Saltley, Bordesley, Bordesley Green, Small Heath and a section of Alum Rock. And on the south they stretched across Highgate, Balsall Heath, Sparkbrook, Greet, some of Tyseley and much of Sparkhill. Additionally, evacuation

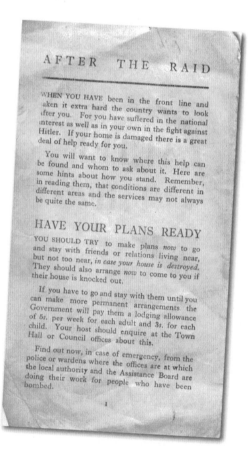

'After the Raid' leaflet issued by the Ministry of Home Security, December 1940, belonging to the Essex family.

was carried on in Bournbrook, Selly Park, Stirchley, Ten Acres and some of Selly Oak.

On 1 September the official evacuation began. John Hawkins evoked the scene, as he and his little sister left St Benedict's School, in Heather Road, Small Heath. Their mother had begun to urge him to mind Rosie, 'and turning abruptly away, her sentence unfinished, she shambled quickly off, to apparently join the crowd of watching parents, as her voice trailed away to a choking whisper'. Then their teacher 'shepherded us both into waiting lines' and handed them their labels. Dutifully, John slipped the bootlace over Rosie's head and stretched his neck to 'try and catch a last comforting glimpse of Mom'. His sister held on to his hand and:

> *Quite suddenly, screeching noisily, the heavy steel railing gates were now swung back, and the nearest lines of children obediently picked up their cases, shouldered their haversacks and gas-masks, and led by their escort of teachers, began to file through them in a long double column. Some parents now ran frantically alongside the long trudging procession, anxiously searching for their own children, and having found them, loudly shouted advice, encouragement, or last-minute instructions, - 'Look arter the nipper now, - we'll be cummin' down ter see yer next wik', or, 'Purra sock in it yer big cry-babby, - they wunt let yer ride a norse if they sees yer in that state yer know!' On we all marched, past the houses, shops and factories that we all knew so well, and from which now poured housewives, overall-clad factory workers, shop assistants, men and women, young and old to loudly cheer us on our way. Firmly and protectively grasping Rosie's hand, laden with a full haversack, and my gas-mask box bouncing gently against my thigh, I strode purposefully on towards Tyseley Station, and the waiting train.* (John Hawkins, *Operation Pied Piper*, unpublished manuscript, n.d., pp. 54-5)

The first evacuation train left Brum at 8.20 a.m., and others followed throughout that day and the next. All journeys began from New Street, Snow Hill or Moor Street stations, and then stops were made at local stations to pick up more evacuees. The children were greeted by wardens and police officers, but ticket inspectors and collectors stopped tearful mothers from joining them on the platforms ('Evacuation Day', *Birmingham Mail*, 1 September 1939). Enid Stainforth was nine years old at the time and she brought to mind how she 'became one of the children standing forlornly on a station platform with my gas mask and my name tag round my neck'. She and the other children were 'shepherded on to the train by the flustered teachers and it only seemed a short time before we were being unloaded again'. (Enid Stainforth, 'Rolls Royce and Rabbit Stew - A Wartime Childhood', unpublished manuscript, n.d., p. 1).

Douglas C. Wilson vividly recollected his journey:

> *Inside a moving railway carriage, set in a dirty ceiling, a light bulb burned creating shadow under the luggage racks, shadow that bright-angled sunbeams cut through to illuminate discoloured wall-prints of lake-side views; and a dull brass plate that indicated the heat was 'on'. Children sat restless on dust impregnated seats their feet scuffing sweet wrappings into spilt lemonade. Respirators hung from their shoulders and on the coats of many - like parcels in the post - were labels displaying names and home addresses. The engine, hissing, stopped. Heads craned from carriage windows, eyes in soot smudged faces scanned the landscape. They saw acres of fruit*

trees, a signal pointing to the sky and along the ballasted track, a bridge; beyond that distant town. The evacuees' journey to safety was almost over. The adventure had begun. (Douglas C. Wilson, *A Child Goes from War*, unpublished autobiographical novel, n.d., p. 49).

The town was Evesham and Douglas remained there for fifteen months, until he was old enough to start work back in Birmingham.

Jim Moon was younger and he was enchanted by his experience of evacuation. He was sent to the village of Henley-in-Arden in Warwickshire. Like his fellows he 'had seen pictures of farms and the country in magazines' but he had never looked at fields of cows and sheep until the train journey. Compared to Moor Street Station, the Henley station was 'such a contrast' as it had 'flower beds and railing at the back and the footbridge'. When the children reached the school 'we were given a large carrier bag made of paper with string handles, which was full of goodies'. It was 'just like Christmas all over again', as there were 'sweets, biscuits and the largest slab of chocolate I had ever seen'. The whole experience was magical 'because everything there was new to us', especially the ability and freedom 'to walk over the fields and pick wild flowers like violets and primroses'. On one occasion a reporter from the Birmingham Mail arrived, bought double ice-cream cones and 'took a photo of a group us in the doorway of the school next to the Ice-Cream parlour'. (Letter, April 1995).

Brummie evacuees outside the ice-cream shop in Henley-in-Arden, 4 September 1939; probably the occasion recalled by Jim Moon of Garrison Lane Schools, Bordesley.

After a few months Jim was brought back to Birmingham by his mom and dad. Unlike him, Jacqueline Simmonds was away from home for much longer. She was nine years old when she was evacuated with her sister Pat to South Wales. After reaching Troy Station, Monmouth, 'we were transported to Brynderi school in the parish of

Llantilio Crosseny to await allocation in our new homes'. Tired and bewildered she was taken to the hamlet of Whitecastle, 'the home of my new-to-be "Auntie and Uncle"'. The upheaval in her life 'was very traumatic but I for one soon settled down to the ways of country life, the peacefulness of which made the air raids on the big cities seem very far away'. Jacqueline was happy at the local school and she was well cared for by her foster parents. She stayed with them for almost five years, until July 1944 when 'I had to return to Birmingham to commence work'. (Letter, 10 June 1995).

Most children spent a much shorter period away from home, and many did not join the evacuation at all. It was estimated that between 80,000 and 90,000 children should have left Birmingham at the start of the war, but the total only reached 25,241 pupils from elementary schools plus 4,260 teachers and helpers, and between 5,000 and 6,000 from secondary schools. They were joined by sixteen blind and four disabled adults, 406 pregnant women, and 4,135 mothers with 7,858 children under five years of age. Most of these were sent to the rural parts of Warwickshire, Worcestershire, Gloucestershire, Herefordshire and Leicestershire. By 31 October 1939, 90% of the mothers had returned to their homes - some doing so on the night that they were evacuated. According to one official:

> It clearly shows how difficult it is to operate a scheme that means the separation of a woman from her husband and home. Another factor has had a great influence on the returns - the nature of the transition from a central area of Birmingham to remote rural districts. Many of the people, of course, are not used to a country life, and felt isolated and miserable. Neither do women like sharing a house. It is not an ideal arrangement. Two women and one gas stove is enough to cause friction in most homes. ('Evacuation from Birmingham', *Birmingham Post*, 31 October 1939).

By this date it was obvious that many children had also returned to Birmingham. They included those who had gone with their schools as well as those like Val Preece, who had been evacuated privately. She attended Alston Road School in Little Bromwich, outside Birmingham's evacuation zone, and 'I remember sitting listening to the radio to that now-famous broadcast by Mr Chamberlain and I asked my parents what war was like'. Soon after the family took charge of an Anderson Shelter but it was never used 'except by frogs', and then Val was packed off to an aunt in Newtown, Montgomeryshire, where she went to school. But the phoney war continued and 'nothing seemed to be happening and so I came home again'. (Letter, 1996). The lull in the war was not the only reason for the marked move back to Brum. Many children were homesick and were missed by their parents. With other children from Rookery Road School, Handsworth, Joan Horspool and her elder sister had been despatched to the village of Belbroughton, Worcestershire. Her separation from her mom and dad and Grandma Davis 'with whom we lived' was traumatic. They returned 'home for an intended short visit', but 'although we were well placed in Belbroughton the upset of being parted from our parents again was so upsetting to all concerned we never went back to our substitute home in the country'. (Letter, 16 February 1995).

Sammy Gregory was one child who made his own mind up to return to Brum. Just ten-years old, he had been sent from St Paul's School, Hockley to Abergavenny in South Wales. From there the children were transported by bus to Llanover:

> where we were taken to the village school and sorted out. I was sent with a lad

called Freddie Jones to Thousand Acre Farm owned by Mr Isaacs. We used to have to go to bed early to help fetch the cows in. We didn't go to the village school as we were kept separate. Our headmaster Mr Bate-Jones stayed in the village with two of our teachers who taught us. I couldn't settle to country life so stayed for just a year. I saved my pocket money and told Freddie Jones I was going home. I got a walloping off my dad for coming home. (Letter, August 1996)

Not all of the evacuees had happy experiences. In some places working-class Brummie children were made unwelcome, whilst others were treated insensitively. ('Children from Birmingham', *Birmingham Mail*, 25 October 1939, and 'Evacuation Pay Up To-morrow', *Birmingham Evening Despatch*, 27 October 1939). Pat Houghton and her brother were two of those who had a difficult time. She was 'thrilled to bits at the journey, because I was seeing the countryside'. But her enjoyment was marred when her party arrived at Retford in Nottinghamshire. They were assembled in the school hall 'and people came in and picked children to take home with them. And nobody wanted a brother and a sister - they were taking them in ones, but children from the same family, it was difficult to place them'. (Interview with Doreen Hopwood, 20 May 1996, p. 12). Mr T. Clarke had a similar experience later in the war. With his two brothers he was evacuated from Twickenham Road School, Kingstanding, 'with all my belongings in a "handy carrier"'. They went to Ripley in Derbyshire, where 'we were "distributed" from a brightly lit school room'. He has only 'very sad memories' of his time away from Birmingham, as he and his brother Len were separated from their other brother Norman. (Letter, 1995).

Cost was a major factor in encouraging a return of evacuees to Birmingham. The Government paid foster parents 9s for the billet of each child, and from 28 October 1939 moms and dads were expected to make a contribution towards this expense. The standard charge was 6s for each child, although the ability to pay was means-tested. This proposal was criticised strongly in

Boys of Turves Green Council School 'digging for victory', cultivating waste land for food production, 13 March 1940.

Birmingham. It was pointed out that 'where there are families of three and four school-children - and large families are the rule rather than the exception in the more congested areas of Birmingham - the Government payments demanded under the evacuation scheme will represent a quarter and a third respectively of the average earnings of the bread winner'. ('Billet Will Hit Thousands of Parents', *Birmingham Evening Despatch*, 5 October 1939). At the end of October 1939 a further 2,000 children were scheduled to leave Birmingham, but the worry over payments meant that 'so few turned up that this second evacuation "dribbled away"'. ('Birmingham's Second Evacuation - Many Did Not Turn Up', Birmingham *Evening Despatch*, 25 October 1939).

With the outbreak of war, 130 children from Garrison Lane Schools, Bordesley had been evacuated to Henley-in-Arden. By Christmas half of them had returned home. ('Putting the Tail on the Pig', *Birmingham Mail*, 30 December 1939). These figures were typical, and the move back to Birmingham accelerated over the holiday period - so much so that by the end of January 1940 at least 93% of elementary school children were back in the city. Unsurprisingly, the evacuation scheme was branded a 'failure'. ('Evacuation', *Birmingham Mail*, 24 January 1940). During the spring of 1940 a new plan was brought in whereby parents were required to register their children for voluntary evacuation in the case of air raids. A few months later there was heavy bombing in the Tyburn area of Erdington, and it was included in Birmingham's evacuation zone. On 25 September, 567 children and 61 adults were moved out.

Two months later the east side of Birmingham was blitzed so badly that it was rendered almost waterless. The risk of epidemics was great and between 26 November and 10 December over 22,000 children were evacuated urgently. Eileen Kerrigan was one of them. She and her brother lived in Cromwell Street, Nechells and 'the night before we were evacuated was particularly bad but early next morning as usual we were out looking for shrapnel with the rest of the kids'. With their school they were sent to Worksop in Nottingham where they were fostered with 'two sisters married to two brothers' who lived next door to each other. Between them they had three boys who were 'the same age as us' and 'the first thing they asked us was if we had any shrapnel. We were very popular then.' (Letter, 7 August 1996).

Bombing continued and had severe effects on parts of the city which were not in the evacuation zone. This was apparent especially in south-western districts of Brum. The city made strong representations to the Ministry of Health and at last the whole of Birmingham was made an evacuation zone. In mid February over 2,000 children were moved to South Wales and rural Staffordshire. This brought to 25,000 the number of children evacuated officially. A similar figure had been moved out privately by their moms and dads. ('50,000 Evacuees', *Birmingham Mail*, 20 February 1941). Rita Dexter was one of those included in these evacuations of the Blitz.

> I attended Holy Souls RC school in Acocks Green, and was about eleven when the bombing started earnestly. We were also without water, this only being delivered by tankers (tea with a hint of petrol - different!). Everyday we said our tearful goodbyes, only to reappear home again at 4.00 p.m. Then it happened, it was for real. We were on the train, destination unknown to us. I now know that we were going to a mining community in Mansfield, Nottingham. The day lost its enchantment when we were all piled into the Village Hall, tired, hungry and bewildered. On reflection, it was really awful. Kindly people came in and chose their evacuee. Not nice when you are among the last three to be selected. It was, I suppose, almost ten at night when a rather severe looking lady chose myself and another girl who I didn't know particularly well. (Letter, 19 September 1994).

Brian Noden was another child who was sent from Birmingham in this later evacuation. He was eight-years old and attended Peckham Road School in Kingstanding. With his older cousin, Gordon Bennett, he boarded the evacuation train at Castle Bromwich Station. He had his obligatory gas mask, 'brown paper carrier bag containing a change of underclothes and a packet of sandwiches', and he remembered that he was 'excited, scared and very, very lonely'. They left the train at Mansfield, and were then put on buses to be billeted in various nearby villages. His overriding memory is of the dedication of his teachers, 'who were as mentally and physically upset by this sudden upheaval, and being thrown as we were into strange environments virtually overnight, who had to go far beyond their normal school duties.' In particular Brian recalled the care of Miss Stinson and Miss Aslin, 'a genie in disguise'. (Letter, 17 January 1996).

Because of the failure of the initial evacuation, schools were re-opened on a voluntary basis in those parts of Birmingham designated 'neutral'. Initially they could do so only if they were provided with shelters. Ridpool Road Schools in Lea Hall was one of the first to comply with the regulation. The first lessons were devoted to A.R.P. drill. ('School with a Difference', *Birmingham Mail*, 2 October 1939). Norma Westwick went through the same routine at Stechford Junior and Infant Schools:

Gas mask practice at Ridpool Road Schools, Lea Hall, 2 October 1939.

I remember well gas mask practice which petrified me. Our school housed the air raid siren in the play ground which had to be heard with a two mile or more radius, so you can imagine how deafening it was when sounding off. When this did happen we were all evacuated to brick built air raid shelters which were partly under ground. We had to clap hands and sing as loud as we could! 'Ten green bottles hanging on the wall' which now when I think about it was a very long song. This way we could not hear the air craft or bombs dropping. (Letter, 14 June 1995).

Schools throughout the 'non-evacuable areas of Birmingham were re-opened compulsorily in May 1940, by which date all of the buildings had shelters. In the 'evacuable' zone of Birmingham, a system of 'Home Teaching' was introduced. Parents lent rooms, accommodation was found in churches and halls, and classrooms were used in schools which officially were closed. Arthur Thorneycroft received his schooling in 'the smoke room of an old pub!' Formerly the 'Rolling Mill Tavern' in Thimblemill Lane, Nechells it had become a cafe owned by the famed Brummie boxer Bert Kirby. Arthur had a great time, 'instead of a third of a pint of milk and a biscuit we had hot toast and tea at break-time!' (Letter, 17 March 1996).

A pupil at St George's, Hockley, Betty Foxall was taught in a similar way. She had not been evacuated because her mom said 'we would all go together if necessary' and she recalled that her education was 'hit and miss: some days the teachers did not turn up for class if they had a bad night or perhaps one teacher would come & meet us in the church & give us some work to do while we were in the shelter'. (Letter, August 1996). Joan Horspool of Handsworth agreed that the war 'had a big effect on our education as a lot of time was lost in the early years and although they were excellent teachers', the majority were middle-aged or elderly'. She was still at school when the war ended and believes that 'my generation missed out on our childhood and were forced to grow up and mature' because of 'the times we lived in'. (Letter, 12 February 1995). More than anything, it was the sights, sounds, feelings and tragedies of the Blitz which robbed many young Brummies of their childhoods.

Schooling at a home in Sutton Coldfield, October 1939.

CHAPTER TWO

BRUM FIGHTS BACK:
THE CALL TO ARMS

A parade of the Birmingham Home Guard receiving the salute of General Sir Robert Gordon-Finlayson, G.O.C. Western Command, in front of the Council House, 23 March 1941. The parade included Bomb Disposal, Medical and Security Sections as well as 'regular' Home Guard battalions.

Escape from Dunkirk: the Fall of France

The phoney war was not completely peaceful. Magnetic mines were laid by the Germans along the coast of Britain and many lives were lost when U-boat submarines sank the aircraft carrier *Courageous* and the battleship *Royal Oak*. But on land, France remained free from attack and the feeling grew that 'Hitler had missed the bus', as Chamberlain put it on 4 April 1940. Sadly, the Prime Minister was proved wrong. Five days after his confident words, the *Wehrmacht* swept into Denmark unopposed and seaborne troops seized Oslo and the other major cities of Norway. In the succeeding battles the German navy suffered heavy losses. Still, by 8 June the Nazis were triumphant and British soldiers were withdrawn from the north of Norway, where they had been sent to combat the *Wehrmacht*.

Dispirited and dejected, Chamberlain resigned as Prime Minister on 10 May - the same day that the Germans invaded Belgium and Holland. He was replaced by

Winston Churchill, a charismatic leader whose radio broadcasts later inspired the people of the United Kingdom when all seemed lost. Three days after coming to office he stirred the nation with a speech in Parliament:

> I would say to the House, as I said to those who have joined this Government: 'I have nothing to offer but blood, toil, tears and sweat'. We have before us an ordeal of the most grievous kind. We have before us many, many long months of struggle and of suffering. You ask what is our policy? I will say: It is to wage war, by sea, land and air, with all our might and with all the strength that God can give to us; to wage war against a monstrous tyranny, never surpassed in the dark, lamentable catalogue of human crime. That is our policy. You ask, What is our aim? I can answer in one word: Victory - victory at all costs, victory in spite of all terror, victory, however long and hard the road may be; for without victory, there is no survival. (Charles Eade, compiled, *The War Speeches of the Rt Hon Winston Churchill*. Volume I, London, no date, p. 181).

The Dutch army was overwhelmed and on 14 May the Germans bombed Rotterdam, killing 900 civilians. By now the *Wehrmacht* was advancing rapidly through France, after concentrating their attacks on weak links in the French defence. This *Blitzkreig*, or lightning war, was so effective that within days France's leading generals were accepting the inevitabilty of defeat. Aware of the impending French collapse, General Gort realised that he had to evacuate the British Expeditionary Force. He pulled his forces back to defensive lines around Dunkirk, aided by the stiff resistance put up by the outnumbered and outgunned Belgian forces. Unable to fight any longer, Belgium surrendered on 27 May and the British withdrawal started. The situation was dire. Everywhere the *Wehrmacht* was rampant and it was feared that only 10,000 British troops would be saved. In the event 200,000 men were brought back home, along with

Mothers at the Carnegie Institute, Hunters Road, Handsworth, receiving free respirator helmets for their babies, 19 September 1939.

140,000 French and Belgian soldiers. Their safety was assured by the actions of the Royal Navy and a flotilla of small boats which sailed to Dunkirk and took men from the beaches. The evacuation was protected by the bravery of pilots from the Royal Air Force, by the courage of 150,000 French troops who became prisoners of war after Dunkirk, and by the resilience of the British Army's rearguard.

Arthur Gunn was one of those saved. He was in an ambulance convoy which went along roads 'littered with dead civilians mown down with machine guns from dive bombers' and with 'shattered horses lying dead, others kicking in pain, wounded'. In the midst of this mayhem and slaughter there was one especially poignant scene of a dead young mother with 'a baby still suckling her breast'. Arthur and his fellows gave the baby to another woman with a child. When their ambulance ran out of petrol, they destroyed its engines with sledge hammers and 'made our way towards Dunkirk, which was ablaze as the oil storage tanks had been bombed'. They were turned away from the port and directed to La Panne. Thousands of men were on the sand dunes and 'surgeons were trying to cope with the wounded, brought in their hundreds due to the non-stop bombing'. Wading into the water to reach the rescue boats, Arthur and the others had to duck 'when the Germans tried to mow us down'. Eventually he grabbed hold of a chain hanging from a Royal Navy motorboat. The vessel was fully loaded 'but I hung on even though they tried to push me off with a boat hook'. A mile out to sea the motorboat reached the SS *Yewdale* and Arthur was taken aboard.

The decks were crowded with troops so we had to go in the hold. I can remember hearing the continuous attacks by dive bombers, and the Lewis gunner on the ship deserved the VC! He never stopped firing. About six o'clock in the evening some bombs struck but somehow God spared us, though a large hole was blown in the hold. There was a blinding flash, shrapnel flew all around, a terrible blast blew my trousers off and a wave of vibration went through my body. I had a chunk of flesh torn from my thigh, and gashes under my chin, on my temple and cuts all over my face. The Frenchman next to me had been killed.

Arthur reached Ramsgate and then spent five weeks at Derby Royal Infirmary. After returning to his unit he had delayed shell shock and following seventeen weeks of treatment he was discharged as unfit for military service. ('Horrors of My Dunkirk Escape', *Evening Mail*, May 1990).

Jack Frizzel was also at Dunkirk. An apprentice at the Austin, he had joined the Territorial Army in April 1939 and was called up as a regular when war was declared. Sent to France, he was a driver in "A" Section of the Royal Army Service Corps Ammunition Company. His unit was based at Plouvain behind the Maginot Line and was moved into Belgium when the German *Blitzkreig* began. During the retreat the men picked up civilians 'against orders, but the plight of many of their wounded moved us to help'. As Jack and his colleagues approached Tournai 'we were shocked at last to see the consequences of war, as it was to become to so many cities later on. Shattered buildings with piled rubble, and rescue workers trying to dig out the dead were on every side as we drove slowly through the dust-laden town'. Abandoning their vehicles, the men marched to Dunkirk and in the chaos were split up. Jack and his mate Fred joined one of the numerous official parties gathered on the beaches. Eventually they lined up in the water and were picked up by HMS *Winchelsea*. (Jack Frizzel, *A Few Days at The Seaside*, unpublished manuscript, 1988).

One Brummie soldier who did not escape home was James Dolman from Nechells. He had joined the Territorial Army as a teenager and when war was declared he was called up as a regular with 9th Battalion, the Royal Warwickshire Regiment. By early January 1940 he was stationed in France as a bren gunner. Soon after his twentieth birthday:

the Germans broke through around the Maginot line and quickly came South. We were suddenly paraded and transported in army lorries into Belgium. Our bren gun carrier was blown up in an air attack by Stukas. We were moved about here, there and everywhere. I think the idea was to create the impression that a large force was present, at least that is what I thought. After spending three days and nights on a dried up canal, of which we were told was the Albert Canal, with just the occasional burst of gunfire, it was the early morning of 24th April when we found ourselves surrounded and we became prisoners of war.

After their capture, James and his mates were lined up 'and were about to start marching when there was a burst of machine gun fire from the right and six of our chaps lay wounded in the legs'. For almost the next five years James endured 'purgatory', imprisoned in Stalag XXA Camp 13 in Poland and having to work on farms for the Germans. In 1943 he escaped, but was recaptured. He was liberated early in 1945. When he returned home he was 'very weak and only six stone, 11 pounds' in weight. (James Alfred Dolman, unpublished manuscript, 1995, pp. 8-23).

The Germans are Coming: The Fear of Invasion

Many men at Dunkirk were saved but much vital equipment was lost, including six destroyers, 177 fighter planes, numerous tanks, guns and vehicles and thousands of rifles. On 15 June the last British divisions in France were withdrawn from Normandy, along with 10,000 Polish troops. The next day Marshall Pètain became the head of a French government. On 21 June he concluded a humiliating armistice with Germany, which was repudiated by General de Gaulle, who set up a Free French government in London. The United Kingdom's situation was dire. Serious defeats had damaged both the nation's confidence and its capacity to fight. France had capitulated. Most of the smaller nations of Europe had been conquered by the Germans or else were cowed by them. Led by Mussolini, Italy had joined the war on the side of Hitler. Stalin was determined to maintain the Soviet Union's non-aggression pact with Germany and the United

RHYMED INFORMATION.

If you get a choking feeling and a smell of Musty Hay,
You can bet your bottom dollar that there's Phosgene on the way,
But the smell of bleaching powder will inevitably mean,
That the enemy you're meeting is the gas we call Chlorine,
When your eyes begin a-twitching and for tears you cannot see,
It's not Mother peeling onions but a dose of C.A.P.
If the smell resembles peardrops, then you'd better not delay,
It's not Father sucking toffee, it's that ruddy K.S.K.
If you catch a pungent odour as you're going home to tea,
You can safely put your shirt on it, they're using B.B.C.
D.M., D.A. and D.C. emanate the scent of roses,
But despite their pretty perfume they ain't good for human noses.
Tho' for garlic or for onions you've a cultivated taste,
When in War you meet those odours leave the area in haste ;
For it's mustard gas, the hellish stuff that leaves you one big blister,
And in hospital you'll need the kind attention of the Sister.
And lastly, while geraniums look pleasant in a bed,
Beware their smell in War time—if it's Lewisite, you're dead.

FIRST-AID TREATMENT.

CHOKING OR LUNG IRRITANTS.

PHOSGENE (C.G.)

Protection. Respirator complete.

NOSE GASES OR ARSENICAL SMOKES.

CHLORINE.

Respirator complete

Card about gas attacks issued to F. E. Hartley of Stoney Lane, Yardley by Serck Radiators, Warwick Road, Greet.

States of America was resolutely neutral. Nazi Germany bestrode Europe. In a continent where evil and despotism were triumphant, the United Kingdom kept alight the beacon of freedom. But in the aftermath of defeat, there were real fears that Hitler would extinguish that flame through invasion.

These worries remained throughout much of 1940, as Sheila Herdman stressed. One night in November her family 'left our house in Small Heath to stay with relatives in the more salubrious area of Quinton'. They hoped for a peaceful night 'for at last we were away from the BSA armaments factory, and the nearby canal which pinpointed its whereabouts to the Luftwaffe with frightening regularity'. Sheila's uncle was due to start fire watching later that night and so he went to bed upstairs, whilst everyone else slept on mattresses downstairs. They were all awoken by a strange noise which increased in tempo and intensity.

> It was not the familiar, dreaded sound of the Luftwaffe's engines, nor the screech of falling bombs, nor the shrill whistle blown by the air raid wardens to denote 'Take cover - direct hit imminent'. It was far worse. Uncle rushed into the dining room, clad in pyjamas, scarf and tin helmet. He grabbed the poker from the fireplace and announced: 'The Germans are attacking the house. I shall defend it against all odds'. He added: 'I fought the buggers on the Somme and I'll fight 'em now'. He was, however, in no hurry to do so, and insisted on making cocoa for us all, while the noise continued. Then someone banged on the door, and shouted through the letter box. Auntie said: 'He's shouting in English, not German - let him in Frank!' So Uncle did so, but took the poker, and a castiron saucepan, just in case. A very British voice said: 'Sorry to bother you, old chap, but our barrage balloon has broken free from its moorings. I'm afraid it's on your roof. The cables can do a lot of damage, and make an awful noise.' A team of RAF men arrived and removed the offending balloon. And then we slept. (Letter, 26 February 1995).

Derek Matthews had a similar experience. He and his brother Fred were evacuated to East Kirby, Nottinghamshire but after six weeks they came home to Coleman Street, Nechells. Living close to the gas works and the railway sheds, the bombing 'got so bad that it was decided that my mom, my Gran (who lived in Great Lister Street) Fred and me would have to go to our weekend bungalow at Holt Fleet that my Grandad had built'. Travelling by two buses and then walking they reached their destination by the River Severn as it was becoming dusk. Before going to their bungalow they stopped at a farm 'for some milk and bread', where 'the talk was of "THE INVASION" that was to come at any time'. The two boys fell asleep only to be woken 'by my Mom & Gran in a very excited state'. They shouted, 'get up quick, the Germans have landed, there's paratroopers at the back', and explained that they had heard planes and seen 'lights flashing in the back fields'. Their nerves were taut from night after night of air raids in Brum, 'where it was a crime to show a light', and they propped the mattresses against the door 'to keep the Germans out'. The next thing Derek remembered 'it was morning' and 'we were still alive'. The family had slept the night against the door. After a discussion and 'something to eat' they went to 'find out what was happening in the world'. At the farm they told Mrs Blick about the Germans.

> She seemed quite amazed at us. There were no Germans she said. The lights we had seen was 'Mr Blick getting some sheep in that had got out'. We stayed a couple of

weeks after that then the old man decided 'if we were going to die, we might as well die together'. As I have wrote this down I feel very sad and at the same time I can't help smiling. Sad that I'm the last one left. My Mom, Gran and brother Fred have all died, and the smile? Well if they had been German Paratroopers how would we have kept them out? The bungalow was only made of match board, the Germans could have put their boots straight through it. (Letter, July, 1996).

A Heinkel bomber which came down at Earlswood, Warwickshire, 11 May 1941. The Home Guard man on the left is Colin North. Four crewmen were on the plane, three were killed and the other was thrown out on fire. He was saved because he fell into a water-filled ditch. Information supplied by Godfrey Nall.

A Citizen's Army: the Home Guard

As the situation in France worsened, the threat of a German invasion became more serious. Warnings were given to cyclists not 'to leave their machines where they could get into the hands of parachute invaders'; motorists were told 'to render their cars unusable at night' for the same reason; and signposts were removed at crossroads. ('Local Defence', *Birmingham Mail*, 21 May 1940; 'Signposts Go', *Birmingham Mail*, 3 June 1939). A more assertive response to the growing threat of a German invasion came on 14 May 1940 when the Government broadcast an appeal for the formation of Local Defence Volunteers. Three months later this body was renamed the Home Guard. It had two main tasks: to protect major work places, railways, canals and other strategic sites; and to deal with parachute invaders and emergencies. In Birmingham the Home Guard was split into groups attached to one of the city's 35 police stations. In addition many factories formed their 'own internal defence units from amongst their workers, and these will be used solely for the defence of the particular premises where they are located'. ('Local Defence', *Birmingham Mail*, 21 May 1940).

William Shaw was one of the men who joined the Home Guard at Walton and Brown's, the cycle component manufacturer's in Downing Street, Handsworth. They were attached to the Royal Warwickshire Battalion, Birmingham and were commanded by J. Barlow, the firm's managing director, whilst the sergeant major was Fred Wade, one of the foremen. Just across the municipal boundary in Smethwick, Avery's also had their own Home Guard unit, whilst men from a number of factories in Ladywood operated a Home Guard Motor Patrol Boat on the nearby canal. (Alan T. Shaw, Letter, 21 May 1995; 'Christening the Home Guard Warship', *Birmingham Mail*, 20 August 1940). On the roof at one 'important works' a look-out tower was built. This 'armoured crow's nest' gave 'an uninterrupted view of the surrounding country'. Each night it was defended by fifteen members of the Home Guard who kept watch in relays. Below the tower was 'a heavy brick-built shelter, provided with look-out or firing embrasures, and in telephonic communications with the works. ('The Spotters', *Birmingham Mail*, 20 September 1940).

Members of the A.F.S. 'Naval Detachment' with a 70 foot fire boat, at practice taking water from a canal, 14 October 1939.

Within a few days 30,000 men had joined the new force in Birmingham. At first 'they were held together by little more than their own enthusiasm and in the early stages records consisted almost solely of lists of names collected at the police stations which served as recruiting centres'. (Black, *History of the Corporation*, p. 91). The men had to parade in their civilian clothes and arms drill was carried out with broom stales because real weapons were so scarce. Gradually things improved. The volunteers were given badges relating to their county regiment and fitted out with denim overalls and then serge battle-dress. By early 1941 they had been provided with rifles and were organised on army lines with non-commissioned and commissioned officers.

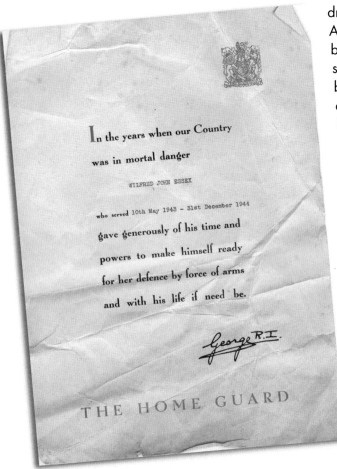

One of them was Ted Gough's dad, a driver of mail vans for the Post Office. An ex-serviceman, he was too old to be called up for the army and he also suffered badly with asthma. Still he became an officer in the Home Guard and 'did his share of fire-watching. He was away so many hours we never knew when or how he would get home. In 1941 he was awarded the Imperial Service Medal for bravery during a very bad night raid on the city centre. We never knew what happened. He just did not want to talk about it.' (Letter, 1995).

There were others like him. Commander George Inwood was the first Home Guard officer to be awarded the George Cross. On 15 October 1940 he was called to a bombed house in Bishop Street. Five people were trapped in a cellar into which gas was escaping. Twice George went into the ruins, each time pulling a person clear. Heedless of his own safety he entered the cellar a third time. He collapsed and died from gas poisoning. (Richard Armstrong, 'The bravest of the brave', *Birmingham Goes to War. 50th Anniversary 1939-1989. Evening Mail Special*, 14 August 1989, p. 10). Later that winter Section Leader A. H. Brunges and Patrol Leader C.W.L. Tozer both gained the George Medal for their valour 'when at great risk to themselves they extricated several persons trapped under wreckage in a basement rapidly filling with water and gas from broken mains. ('Home Guard Heroes', *Birmingham Mail*, 2 October 1941).

Home Guard Certificate awarded to Wilfred Essex of Kings Norton, a worker at Webley and Scott's gunmakers, Weaman Street.

The bravery of such men belies the image of the Home Guard as a 'Dad's Army' whose members were nervy and incompetent. There were many older men in the force, but most of them were ex-servicemen who were familiar with weapons and who provided a voice of experience for their younger fellows. And a significant proportion of the volunteers were members of gun clubs and knew how to shoot. By 1941 the Home Guard had become not only a significant element in Birmingham's civil defence but also a well-trained fighting force. In July of that year they were engaged in a successful full-scale exercise in which they had to defend Birmingham against invasion, and soon after they were supplied with new anti-tank weapons. In 1942 the Birmingham Battalion 'led the country' by forming the first Women's Auxiliary, and from March of that year, 7,000 of them served with anti-aircraft batteries. ('The Invasion of Birmingham', *Birmingham Post*, 14 July 1941).

Tom Wareing was one of these ack-ack gunners. At fourteen he had become a police messenger based at Billesley Police Station. A year later and under age he joined the Home Guard anti-aircraft unit at Stonehouse, Bartley Green. Officially this was '138th (101 Warks HG) Z (M) Anti-Aircraft Battery, Royal Artillery'. After work in the evenings, Tom and his mates were trained by regular soldiers and attended Sunday Parade. He qualified as a gunner 'in six weeks flat' and 'was issued with uniform, battledress, greatcoat, forage cap and R.A. cap-badge . . . boots, ammo, anklets web (unlike the infantry Home Guard) service respirator, steel helmet, shoulder titles - including the Ack-Ack Command Sign - a bow and arrow pointing vertical on a red square background'. (C.T. Wareing, *Dear Sir/Madam. The Life Story of a Frustrated Scribe*, Studley, 1995, pp. 24-5). At its peak the Home Guard in Birmingham numbered 53,000 volunteers. When all danger of invasion had passed they were stood down. With justifiable pride they paraded through the streets of Brum on Sunday, 3 December 1944. (Black, *History of the Corporation*, p. 92).

Restrictions and Arrests: the Internment of 'Aliens'

One final precaution was taken against invasion - the supervision of 'aliens' who were thought to sympathise with the enemy. In September 1939 tribunals were set up and Germans and Austrians were categorised: those in 'A' were arrested immediately and put into internment camps; those in 'B', had their movements restricted; whilst those in 'C' were allowed freedom. Eight months later the clamour grew for more 'aliens' to be interned. This furore was prompted by the appearance of German collaborators in Norway, Denmark and the Netherlands. In response the Government stated that all people in category 'B' were to be arrested. On 26 May 1940, 'just under 100 women aliens' were 'rounded up' in Birmingham. They included 'girls who had been working as domestic servants', wives of male internees, and 'one or two children, looking very puzzled'. As they arrived at New Street Station in their buses, they 'gazed out a little pathetically'. ('Women Enemy Aliens', *Birmingham Mail*, 26 May 1940). Unfortunately and unfairly, some Jewish refugees were arrested - although they were taken to Thorp Street barracks by friendly and courteous policemen. (Josephs, *Survivors*, p. 98).

Mussolini's entry into the war meant that Italians were also interned. Pip Mattiello was one of them. He had been a teenager when he had left Naples for England in 1898 and since then he had lived in Birmingham's Italian Quarter around Duddeston Row, Digbeth. His children were all Brummies, his two daughters were nurses, one of his sons was a lorry driver and the other two, Mick and Joe, were in the armed services. They were outraged at the arrest of their dad and:

> *what we did was went and seen our individual welfare officers and in no time at all*
> *the old man was out. Most of 'em come out because they were all old Italians and*

Joseph Mattiello centre with Carmen Tamburro on the right. The children are Carlo, Michael, Joe, Win and Vera Mattiello and Stevie Tamburro.

they let him out. 'Cus I got a leave on the new year and I got home and the old man says, 'Why don't you and Our Mick mind your own business', he says, 'there I was interned with me mates. They took us to Paignton, then they took us to the Isle of Man, playing with me mates, nothing to do, no work', y'know just playing cards and draughts all day, he says, 'You get me out. I come back here, if I aint down the air raid shelter I'm on nights at the Austin.' (Carl Chinn Show, *BBC Radio WM, 2 May 1995).*

In Birmingham as elsewhere, Italians were still subject to restrictions. They were not allowed to have a radio, they were supposed to abide by a curfew, and their houses were searched regularly by the police. Such visits were not carried out maliciously, but they were irritating and irksome. The loyalty of Brummie Italians was beyond question. Most of them had sons and daughters in the armed forces, whilst some had relatives fighting the Germans in Italy. The Devotis were noted in Birmingham for their confectionery. Before the war one of them, Antonio, had returned to their village - Santa Maria del Taro in Parma. This was an area where the Partisans were active. Following one successful attack, the Nazis vengefully shot dead sixteen villagers. Twenty-three others were arrested, including Antonio. He was sent to a concentration camp, but escaped and hid in the mountains before returning home. His biggest disappointment was that 'the R.A.F. would not accept him when war was imminent in 1939'. (Letter from Eugene Devoti to Rose Devoti, 1991).

Like their fellow Brummies, Birmingham's Italians were affected badly by German air raids. Their quarter was focused on Bartholomew Street, close to the city centre. It was bombed throughout the war, but the worst raid occurred at the end of the Blitz.

At 1.30 a.m. on the 28th July 1942 Antonio and Carolina Bastianelli and her sister Laura were all blown to pieces by a German bomb . . . The air raid shelter in which they had taken refuge received a direct hit. There were six bombs dropped at the same time. Normally the Shelter would have been full with the rest of the residents of Duddeston Row, now Albert Street, and the people from Bordesley Street and also the people who worked at Curzon Street Railway Station. But for one reason or another they hadn't made it to the shelter. The air raid shelter was on waste ground opposite the shops of Bastiannellis and Mattiellos. (Beattie Eastment, Letter, 20 August 1996, information supplied by Hetty Bashford, then Bastianelli).

Working For Victory: War Work

If people were to defend their country they had to have something to fight with, and the wars of the 1930s had shown the importance not only of conventional weapons but also of planes and vehicles. As early as 1935, the Government had decided on a rapid expansion of the military aircraft industry and had begun to fund the building of 'shadow factories'. These produced engines and airframes and were managed by major motor vehicle firms. Birmingham and Coventry were the centres of car making in the United Kingdom and by 1938 all but one of the new engine-producing plants were in these two cities. Later, other shadow factories were built elsewhere, but the significance of the West Midlands was undiminished. In a secret paper written before Dunkirk, the Chiefs of Staff had told Churchill that 'Germany could not gain complete air superiority unless she could knock out our Air Force, and the aircraft industries, some vital portions of which are concentrated at Coventry and Birmingham'. (Winston S. Churchill, *The Second World War. Volume II. Their Finest Hour*, London, 1949, p. 79).

Women hand-sewing Spitfire rudders at the Castle Bromwich Shadow Factory.

Rover built shadow factories at South Yardley and Solihull, where parts for the Bristol Hercules engine were made; whilst the Austin constructed their new plant by their existing works at Longbridge. The preparations for war were extensive. Deep shelter tunnels gave protection to 15,000 workers, 120 acres of glass roof were blacked out, A.R.P. personnel were trained, a Home Guard unit was set up, and both buildings were hidden cunningly. D. Harrison lived in Rednal and 'the view of the Austin from the top of Cofton Park was unbelievable. You couldn't tell there was a factory. It was like a field and trees, an extension of the park. The camouflage was marvellous.' (Letter, August 1996). Fortunately, the Austin was attacked just once and the *Luftwaffe* failed to hinder production. During the war the 'shadow' turned out 2,866 planes such as Fairey Battles, Hurricanes, Stirlings and Lancasters as well as 56,485

Mercury and Pegasus engines and engine sets. Mr R. Jenkins was one of those who made these machines.

> *We were working 2 p.m. till 10 p.m. at the time of the Birmingham air raids and night after night about 6 or 7 p.m. the air raid warnings would sound and the majority would make their way to the shelters. However, the planes were constructed with plywood and a very special kind of glue and once we had started glueing the sections together it had to be finished, come what may. All lights were extinguished when the warnings sounded, and sometimes we finished our operations by torchlight.*
> (April 1940. *Evening Mail Special*, April 1981, p. 5).

Women war workers in Birmingham.

The main Austin factory was as busy as its 'shadow'. Each week it sent out almost 500 army and other vehicles - including ambulances, fire engines, troop carriers and gun tractors. A multitude of other goods poured out of the gates: hydraulic motors for gun turrets; Horsa glider fuselages; balloon cable cutters; oil and fuel tanks for four-engined bombers; components for Rolls Royce engines; exhaust rings for Bristol aero engines; tails for bombs; Vickers and Hispano machine gun magazines; armour-piercing ammunition; ammunition boxes; magazines for tommy guns; service helmets - made on presses previously used for making panels for car bodies; steel helmets for fire watchers; and driving gear units for Churchill tanks. The Longbridge works were as vital to the success of the Royal Navy, producing marine engines for lifeboats, 110,000 magazines for Oerlikon anti-aircraft guns, depth charge pistols and hemisphere pressings and mechanism plates for mines. (*How Longbridge Spanned the Years of War. Austin War Production in Pictures*, Birmingham, 1946, p. 4, thanks to Mr D. B. Adams).

The last shadow factory was constructed by Morris, part of the Nuffield Organisation, at a new plant covering 345 acres in Castle Bromwich - now the Castle Vale Estate.

From May 1940 it was managed by Vickers. Four years later its workers were making 320 Spitfires and 20 Lancasters a month - more aircraft than any other factory in the United Kingdom. In total they produced over 11,000 Spitfires and 300 Lancasters. ('Midland Aircraft Production', *Birmingham Post*, 11 May 1945). An air field was next to the shadow factory. It was the base of 605 Squadron whose members mostly were from Birmingham. They took part in the Battle of Britain and were moved to Croydon on 7 September 1940. Late in 1941 they were sent to East Asia where they were captured by the Japanese. Many of them died. The squadron's colours and memorial are in St Cuthbert's Church, Castle Vale. (Patricia Chapman, Letter, 1 July 1996).

Nuffield was responsible for a number of other important factories in Birmingham, including S.U. Carburettors of Warwick Road, Greet. Carburettors supply engines with petrol and up to the Battle of Britain 'all the aero-carburettors for the R.A.F.'s Spitfires and Hurricanes' were made at this one factory in Brum. If the works had been destroyed 'Britain would have been unable to put into the air any new fighters for a period of at least twelve months. The R.A.F. would have suffered a mortal blow.'

So significant was the factory that it was protected by a 40 foot tall observation tower, two-storey high strongposts and a Home Guard unit provided with an armoured car, machine guns and rifles. After Dunkirk the Government asked the managers and workers to double their weekly output of 100 carburettors. They did so, each of them collaring for at least 77 hours a week. So tired were they that they 'almost dozed at their machines', and when they did sleep it was 'for a few hours' dreamless slumber on couches in the office, or on sacks in a corner of the toolroom'. On 19 November 1940 the factory was hit, but the blaze was put out by the works fire brigade. Two days later great damage was done by girders and debris blasted from adjacent buildings which were blown up. The Air Ministry sent orders for the factory to be abandoned. Production was moved to Shirley where the number of workers was doubled to 1,500. (Ernest Fairfax, *Calling All Arms*, London, 1945, pp. 94-6).

Testing a bullet-proof tyre,
probably at Fort Dunlop, Erdington, 15 December 1939.

Many other firms were involved in making goods for warplanes. In Rea Street, Fisher and Ludlow's produced Lancaster wings, shell cases and bomb tails; Reynold's Tubes of Tyseley manufactured Spitfire wing spans and light alloy tubing; the G.E.C. at

Witton turned out plastic components and much more; whilst Serck Radiators on the Warwick Road, Greet, made all the radiators and air coolers for the Hurricanes and Spitfires which defeated the *Luftwaffe* in the Battle of Britain. And from Fort Dunlop in Erdington there rolled hundreds of thousands of tyres and wheels as well as countless rubber boots and cycle and motorbike rims. ('Dunlop's Part in Victory', *Birmingham Mail*, 31 December 1945). Billy Palmer was at the factory on the night of 11 April 1941. When the sirens wailed he and his mates were sent to the shelters. They were approached by a colleague who was looking for volunteers to fight a fire in Tyre 1 department. The works brigade was unable to do so because it was tackling another blaze.

> *Six of us followed this fellow to Tyre 1 where we were met by Mr George Price who hurriedly put our names on paper: Ernie Cross, Alf Powell, Bill Dutton, Bill Webster, George Peckett and myself. The roof was well alight and naptha pots were exploding. I am sure George Price saved Dunlop from a real disaster that night. George Peckett was injured by falling debris and all of us were soaked and blackened by the smoke from burning rubber. We returned to work after 2½ hours still wet through.* (April 1941. *Evening Mail Special*, April 1981, p. 6).

In Formans Road, Tyseley a plant of Joseph Lucas was an especially dangerous place to work in an air raid. On the site there was a large amount of molten metal, used for lead casting, moulding and die casting. Previously a stores, it became a 'shadow' factory producing Boulton and Paul hydraulic gun turrets for aircraft. Fuel injection equipment was made at a nearby factory in Shaftmoor Lane, but the main Lucas works were in Great King Street, Hockley. This manufactured a variety of goods crucial to the war effort. They included electrically operated traversing gear for

Workers at Joseph Lucas, Great King Street, Hockley. Foreman Jack Turvey is on the right foreground.

rotating gun turrets; rotary transformers for feeding wireless sets on aeroplanes; small bombs which dangled from the cables of barrage balloons; Spitfire wing sub-assemblies; primers and fuses; anti-aircraft shells; mortar bombs; delayed action mechanisms; PIAT anti-tank gun bombs; PIAT anti-tank guns; bayonets; and sten gun magazines. Lucas was also responsible for pioneering work on the combustion and fuel systems of the gas turbines for the Gloster Meteor, the first production jet aircraft. (Harold Nockolds, *Lucas. The First 100 Years. Volume 2. The Successors*, Newton Abbott, 1978, pp. 13-84).

The development of rotating tank gun-turrets had taken place under the supervision of Oliver Lucas. For a time he was also Controller of Tank Design and Development with the Ministry of Supply and was responsible for a collaboration which produced the Cromwell. Rolls Royce made the engines, but the heavy duty cruiser tanks themselves were manufactured by the Metropolitan-Cammel Carriage and Wagon Company at the Midland Works in Washwood Heath and at the Old Park Works in Wednesbury. The Met's other tanks included the Valentine, the Comet and the Tetrarch, whilst the firm also turned out flat wagons for howitzer equipment and tank wagons for aviation spirit. The Saltley Works of the company played as significant a role. It was the leading supplier of radar vehicles and also manufactured components and spares for tanks. Nearby, the Morris Commercial factory at Adderley Park sent out a multitude of vehicles - from standard infantry trucks to wireless and A.A. detector lorries, from light armoured cars to travelling platforms for mobile Bofors guns, and from Crusader tanks to amphibious craft.

In the mid-1930s the chief engineer of the Morris Commercial had gone to Germany and Italy to investigate vehicle designs, purchasing some trucks for shipment back to Birmingham. Soon after he went to Abyssinia and Egypt to study the effect of sand on the engines of Army trucks. He found that it 'simply chewed up the metal into fine particles'. As a result he devised air cleaners 'to prevent the ingress of sand through intake breathers, and generally sealed off all sensitive parts'. Skilled fitters from Birmingham were sent to Cairo where they carried out the modifications to existing vehicles. This development was crucial in the later British successes in North Africa - and so was Morris's shift from six-wheeled to four-wheeled vehicles. The company was as significant in training, and officers and men from cavalry regiments were instructed in Birmingham from 1934. (Fairfax, *Call to Arms*, pp. 98-106).

A Birmingham made tank, tested by driving at full speed over 'sleepers', 15 December 1939.

Both the Lucas at Great King Street and the Morris Commercial were hit by bombs. So was the Wolseley factory at Drews Lane, Washwood Heath. In 1937 its workshops had been inspected by government officials 'in case of emergency, and after that they were left severely alone'. Like the Morris, the Wolseley was part of the Nuffield Organisation, and Lord Nuffield himself had sought the support of the government to involve his firms in rearmament. His efforts were in vain and the writer Ernest Fairfax has declared 'the failure of the Government at that time to mobilise industry earlier was a first-rate disaster'. When hostilities were declared most peace-time production was suspended at the Wolseley, as it was in the majority of Birmingham firms. Workers were laid off everywhere - at Drews Lane alone they numbered 2,000, half of the workforce. The Wolseley's sales manager was sent to London to find out what the company could do for the nation. He returned with an order to make 50,000 percussion fuses for heavy shells each week. Workers were taken on and more contracts followed for sea mines and sinkers, depth charge pistols in phosphorus bronze, gears and suspensions for Cruiser tanks, and 20-mm cannon shot and armour piercing nose caps for Spitfires and Hurricanes. (Fairfax, *Call to Arms*, pp. 106-13; 'Sea Mines Were "Made in Birmingham"', *Birmingham Post*, 28 March 1945).

By the middle years of the war the Wolseley had 1,000 more machines than in peacetime, and its workforce had swelled to over 5,000 people. As at other places, many of the new workers were women. Some of them had responded to recruitment drives, others had been directed from their normal employment locally. One of them was Madelaine M. Sweeney, then Essex. She was head cashier at the Dolcis Shoe Company on the corner of Corporation Street and Bull Street and was sent from there to become 'a final viewer of under-carriages of aircraft' at Styles Developments in Cranmore Boulevard, Shirley. On her first day she was asked could she work with 'a mike (a micrometer)?' She replied 'I'd work with anybody to help the war effort!' (Letter, 10 July 1996). Evelyn Duncan of Kingstanding was another munitions worker. In mid-September 1941 she 'broke the world's individual shell production record'. The next week her factory was visited by Sir Winston Churchill. Evelyn presented the Prime Minister with a box of cigars 'decorated with a large Victory "V"'. Inside was a message which read, 'To our very own Winston, from one of Birmingham's war-work girls. Your example inspired my world's production effort.- Evelyn Duncan.' ('Premier's Visit', *Birmingham Mail*, 27 September 1941; Churchill, *The Second World War*. Volume II. p. 333).

Parade of over 500 women workers aiming to recruit other women for war work, 6 September 1939. The oldest participant was Mary Ann Cottrill, a hand-press operator for parts for planes. She had worked at her factory for 64 years. The parade included almost 100 floats provided by Birmingham firms, showing their contribution to the war effort.

Because of the labour shortage in Birmingham, single people were registered for war work and sent to the city from other parts of the country. They included Phyllis Dutton, then Plendereith, of Earlswood. Her mom and dad would not let her join either the armed forces or the land army and so she was directed to work at Wilmot Breeden in Amington Road, Hay Mills. The factory usually made motor accessories but was now manufacturing Spitfire wings. Phyllis was employed in a 'huge shop' where she and other young women 'filed the rough edges off metal pressings'. Once the wings were produced, they were sent on to Castle Bromwich where the planes were assembled. (Letter to Brian Henderson, 1996). Many youngsters travelled to Birmingham from further distances, having left Northern Ireland, Scotland, South Wales, the South coast of England and the North East. Amongst them was Victor E. Moore from Belfast. Eighteen-years old, he had digs at Stechford and like his fellow lodgers 'was accountable to the National Services Officer at the Labour Exchange' who had 'great powers'. (Letter, 2 February 1995; 'For Munition Workers', *Birmingham Post*, 13 February 1941).

Kath Hendry, then Shields, also came to Birmingham. A Catholic from Lanarkshire, Scotland, she had experienced religious discrimination at home:

> When war was declared I was in service and I was called up. So I had to go into the forces and so I chose Birmingham. Well ma brother came first . . . In Scotland they was very funny about employing Catholics . . . Then when I got my first job in Birmingham I didn't know factory work and I worked on the lathes making shells. Well, I thought this woman was going to ask ma religion after she'd started me. And as I turned away I thought she would call me back. Never even asked ma religion. And this other woman said, 'They're not like that down here. They're not bothered about your religion.' I really thought that was great. (Interview, 1993).

Kath worked at the Birmingham Small Arms Company in Small Heath. In 1936 the Government instructed the company to shift from cycle and motorbike production to the manufacture of guns and following Dunkirk the workers went on a seven-day week. They turned out 50% of all the precision weapons made in the United Kingdom, specialising in the manufacture of Browning aircraft machine guns, Sten guns, Lee Enfield Short Mark III rifles and 20mm Oerlikon cannon. They also provided motor bikes for despatch riders. As with the Lucas at Great King Street, the importance of the B.S.A. was recognised by the *Luftwaffe* and its premises were marked out on maps issued to enemy bombers. They hit their target on 26 August 1940 and although no lives were lost, 750 vital machine tools were destroyed. On that occasion and on 22 October damage was done to the Sparkbrook Works in Montgomery Street, where the machine tools were produced. Fortunately a new factory had been opened at Kitts Green, on the outskirts of Birmingham, where production was uninterrupted.

On 19 November disaster struck the main plant in Armoury Road. Bombs hailed down on Small Heath and Sparkbrook and numerous fires lit up the works, distinctive because of the four-stories of the New Building. The workers were ordered into the shelters. At 9.25 p.m. a low-flying plane dropped two explosives on the structure, and the southern end of the New Building 'disintegrated in a roaring landslide of concrete, machinery, and twisted girders, with dust and black smoke blotting out the details'. ('1861-1961. BSA Centenary', *BSA Group News*, no. 17, June 1961, pp. 36-7, thanks to Barry J. Talboys). Fire fighters, rescue teams and first-aid workers rushed to the ruins which were beginning to blaze. They found that many workers were trapped 'in what had been the ground floor of the outside block', and they had to dodge ammunition which was exploding.

By 10.30 p.m. the firm's fire brigade had been joined by men from 60 other crews. Desperately striving to stop the flames spreading to the rest of the New Building, they pumped water from the Birmingham and Warwick Canal. At the same time rescuers frantically looked for a way to reach the entombed workers. Using his rifle as a crowbar, Albert Bailey and two other Home Guard men prised a way through the mass of rubble to save five men and a woman. Albert went back into the hole he had made and heard voices from the other side of a huge slab of concrete. He managed to force a gap in it, and shining his torch through it he saw four men and a girl. With a bar of iron he enlarged the hole, but a steel girder stopped him from making it big enough for the survivors to crawl through.

Albert was joined by Arthur Stevens, an electrician who wielded oxy-acetyline cutting apparatus. With the fire burning ferociously above them and with smoke gagging them, the two men toiled to make progress. As they worked, other rescuers clambered into the hole and played water upon them. At last it was possible for the trapped workers to scramble out. The woman was farthest from the gap, but in an amazing act of gallantry the men insisted that she was saved first. They flattened themselves on to the floor so that she could crawl over them. Covered 'from head to foot in a black mess of oil and water' she escaped. But the exit was too narrow for

The ruins of the Sydenham Cabinet Company, Moseley Road, Balsall Heath, 27 August 1940. The name of the factory is just visible over the gate and there is writing on the pillar beside it. This information was erased by the censor in the copy of the photograph which was published in the Birmingham Mail on 28 August.

the men. Arthur cut the girder again, whilst Albert protected him from falling masonry. Both of them were scalded because the water which doused them was boiled by the flames. Gradually, they increased the size of the cavity and the men scrabbled out. As the last of them escaped 'there was a rumble and the hole was filled with a mass of blazing wreckage'.

Exhausted, Albert Bailey collapsed and was taken to an ambulance. Arthur Stevens joined rescuers elsewhere. Ignoring the danger, laboriously they dug towards the spot from which shouts had come. They formed a human conveyor belt, along which pieces of steel and masonry were passed. By the time they had gone five feet, Arthur was upside down and his ankles were held by Arthur Harris and Alfred Goodwin - two other electricians. Through a gap in the girders they spotted a man and a woman held fast beneath a heavy wooden bench. For more than four hours Arthur struggled to make space. Occasionally he had to stop whilst water was sprayed on to the trapped workers to stop their clothes smouldering. This was done by two more electricians, T. Hoof and Norman Finlow, and a Home Guard sergeant, Joseph Topham. Eventually, Arthur approached the bench and was able to saw it in half. One section was pulled free by the rest of the rescue team. Once again the woman was farthest from safety. And once again a Brummie working man showed his chivalry. He rolled over to allow the woman to escape before him. In doing so his overcoat became entangled in the debris and he was unable to take it off. Arthur went upside down and two other rescuers tugged at his feet as he grabbed the trapped man under his armpit. As the survivor was pulled out, the hole caved in.

One of the last people rescued was Mr T.F. Hiley. After the bombs hit the New Building he was knocked unconscious whilst sitting on a bench. When he awoke he was beneath the curved part of a steel girder which had crushed to death the two men who had been beside him. The girder was keeping a mass of debris from falling on him, but one of his feet was held fast by a piece of steelwork. After an hour's struggle he freed himself, but 'it seemed that I was no better off, that we were all doomed'. Some people were shouting for help, others were groaning but as flames spread 'their cries were stilling into the strange hush of death'. Mr Hiley found some protection beneath a machine which had formed an arch when it had fallen. Smoke was drawn into his throat, water from hoses trickled upon him and one of his boots began to smoulder. He began to lose hope and thought of knocking himself out so that he would not feel his death. But his instinct for self-preservation asserted itself and he abandoned the idea. He found his pipe, filled it with tobacco and lit it. Occasionally he shouted, but it was exhausting - and yet the silence was terrifying. Then he heard voices and he called to them. After much work, the rescuers cut away the twisted metal and machinery above him, making a narrow exit. Dropping him a rope, they pulled him to safety. It was 5.45 a.m. Mr Hiley had been entombed for nine hours. (Donovan M. Ward, *The Other Battle. A History of the Birmingham Small Arms Co. Ltd*, York, 1946, pp. 48-54).

When Arthur Stevens returned home he did not relate his heroism and he was told off by his wife for 'getting his clothes all messed up'. Both he and Albert Bailey were awarded the George Medal for their bravery. Alfred Goodwin and Arthur Harris were presented with the British Empire Medal, as was Sergeant Joseph Topham. Two other people were honoured similarly - Albert Slim and Corporal John Beattie, who five times went into the wreckage and saved people. The matron of the works, Miss Ada Deeming, became a Member of the British Empire. Fifty-three people were killed that terrible night of 19 November. One of them was the dad of Jean Tyler. Edward Tucker was 36 years old and lived in South Yardley. He worked with a neighbour and the two families shared the same shelter.

> Soon Mr Smart's face appeared at the shelter door, 'They have hit the factory, don't worry I have run all the way home and Eddie will be following.' But that was not to be, and what followed was five dreadful days of waiting and hoping while the rescue work went on. I remember how lots of people kept coming back without good news. I remember Mom losing hope on Friday 22nd when they hit the factory again. On the Sunday lunchtime a police man came and he didn't have to say anything, Mom just shouted, 'I knew it!' From then the neighbours took over us children until we all went to stay with an Aunt and Uncle in Water Orton.

The afternoon on which he was killed, Edward had gone with his wife, Carrie, to buy Christmas presents for their children. (Letter, July 1996).

On 22 November bombs damaged the Waverley Works in Small Heath, a dispersal factory in Tyseley and yet again the main B.S.A factory. As explosives and incendiaries pelted down, the roof spotters continued to look out for planes and to pass on vital information about fires. Their bravery was matched by that of Private William Saragine of the Home Guard. At Armoury Road the internal and external telephone systems were put out of action and extra fire fighters were needed urgently. William volunteered to fetch them. Three times he was thrown from his motorbike by bomb blasts. On another occasion he ran into overhead tramwires which had been blown to the road. They

Alec Henshaw, a renowned peace-time pilot, performing a 'Victory Roll' in a Spitfire above Baskerville House, Broad Street, 18 September 1940. Below is a Messerschmitt brought down in Sussex. The event was in aid of the Lord Mayor's Spitfire Fund. A Birmingham Post reporter described Henshaw's performance as 'a war dance in the air, a manifestation of the R.A.F.'s unconquerable spirit, gay and grim'. Henshaw was the chief test pilot at the Castle Bromwich Shadow Factory and tested more than 3,000 Spitfires.

were live and the volunteer was saved from electrocution only by the rubber of his boots and his tyres. He was awarded the British Empire Medal. No-one died in this raid, but 1,600 machine tools were destroyed or damaged - more than were lost in the whole of Coventry when that city was blitzed on 14 November. Within weeks, the B.S.A. was sending out guns once again from its shattered works, from its plant in Redditch and from a large number of new dispersal factories. (Ward, *The Other Battle*, pp. 57-8).

The B.S.A was not the only factory hit by the Germans. So was one of the premises of Turner Brothers. This firm made a wide range of jigs and tools which were vital in the manufacture of Spitfires, Avro Lancasters, Fairey Barracudas, Hawker Typhoons, Short Stirlings, Bristol Beaufighters, de Haviland Mosquitos, Gloster Jet Planes and other aircraft. Their products were as important in the making of jerricans, tanks, mine detectors, naval gun parts, pontoon bridges, steel lifeboats and Sten guns. (*The War and Turner Brothers*, Birmingham, no date, thanks to Leslie James). They had six sites all close to each other - four in Cleveland Street, one in Hanley Street and another in Hospital Street. This latter factory was remembered for tragic reasons by Vera Ellis.

> I was nine, my eldest brother was fourteen, another one was twelve and I'd got a sister four. So it was hard times . . . It was November the 19th, it was a big incendiary bomb, from what I can remember . . . And he was a working at Turner Brothers, by Tower Street Park, a little factory there, and he was a builder by trade and he used to do this like of a night. All the men used to get stuck in hadn't they. And unfortunately he was up on the roof, or going up on the roof apparently and he got blown off. Killed instantly. But it took me mom five days to find him 'cus there was that many deaths and injuries, people dint know where their loved ones had gone sort of thing . . . She found him at an undertaker's at Dudley Road, after a bit of searching . . . We were shepherded to relations while mom, with a bit of support from her family, went round searching. 'Cus she wouldn't rest, she wasn't going to let him have a communal anything. She wanted her Bill, where she wanted him.

After his death, Bill Stephenson's family were bombed out of their house at 7 back of 14, William Street North, Summer Lane. Friends working at Mitchell's and Butler's, Cape Hill spoke for them and they rented one of the firm's cottages in Wellington Street, Winson Green. They had to move out again temporarily when the nearby Tizer factory was bombed in April 1941. (Carl Chinn Show, *BBC Radio WM*, 25 August 1996).

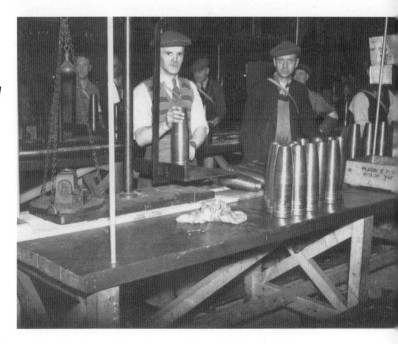

Brummie workers producing cases for anti-aircraft shells, 4 October 1939.

The same raid caused a number of deaths at the Parkinson and Cowan stove factory in Stechford, which was now making ammunition cases, shells, hand grenades, bomb cases and jerricans. Thomas Barnes was at work that night 'when there was a tremendous crash and incendiary bombs came through the roof into the press shop'. He and his mate, Taffy Shapter, dashed outside and went to help fight the blaze which had started in the paint department. There was no pressure behind the water and 'coughing and choking' they had to leave their hose before they were overcome. Both of them were in the Home Guard and they offered their services to 'Wally, the N.C.O.'. He sent them to contact Ernie Watson, who was on duty at the main gate. They found him 'clutching his abdomen with his hands' which were covered with blood. Thomas and Taffy sped off to fetch a first-aid worker. As they did so a bomb exploded close to them. Shrapnel and masonry fell upon them and they were injured. Ernie and Thomas recovered. Taffy died and was buried with full military honours. (April 1941. *Evening Mail Special*, April 1981, p. 6).

One important Birmingham business was bombed out three times. Eddystone Radio was based at the Balmoral Works in Bromsgrove Street. The premises were wrecked in October 1940, although a special condenser for high frequency equipment was saved. It was moved to the Globe Works in Kent Street, the headquarters of the parent company Jarrett, Rainsford and Laughton. This firm made small wares, such as fancy metal goods and face powder compacts, but now it was producing components for shells and mines as well as detonator tubes, primers, pins, and plugs. Its main building was destroyed on 19 November and three days later another of the firm's premises was blown up. Fortunately the condenser was saved on both occasions and after a frantic search, a new location was found at 'the Bath Tub', a lido in West Heath. This site was requisitioned by the Air Ministry which was keen for the research on the condenser to carry on. The outdoor pool was drained, air-raid shelters were built, power presses were brought in and Laughton's resumed its war work whilst Eddystone Radio began to turn out condensers, high frequency chokes, short wave receivers and VHF radio telephone sets for the armed services. Fittingly it was an Eddystone two-way radio transmitter which signalled the beginning of the D-Day landings in June 1944. (*A Century of Achievement. The Story of Laughton & Sons Ltd, 1860-1960*, York, 1960, thanks to Len Smith).

Important wireless work was also carried on at the Monitor Radio Company of Stechford, based in the factory of Parkinson and Cowan. Frank Flanner's research has indicated that the firm was involved in the design, manufacture and assembly of clandestine equipment such as 'the AP5 Transmitter/Receiver, 50 Watt Amplifiers (big in those days) and Eureka Beacons'. The radio sets were produced under the guidance of Polish technicians and were used by British intelligence services to maintain contact with European Resistance fighters. In turn, the partisans utilised the beacons to guide Allied bombers to their targets, whilst the amplifiers directed landings in enemy territory. (Frank Flanner, Radio in WW2 Birmingham, unpublished manuscript, 1992).

An array of Birmingham manufacturers were involved in war work. B.S.A.'s guns often used ammunition made at I.C.I's Kynoch Works in Witton. As early as 1937 the factory had to limit external sales 'so as to clear the way for the Government's defence requirements'. A shadow facility was built as was a full-scale aluminium unit at Holford, Witton. In contrast to the experience of Nuffield but similar to that of B.S.A., I.C.I. was encouraged to prepare for war. The company was 'very closely in touch with the Government on likely requirements of small arms ammunition, and as a result a scheme involving the complete modernisation and rearrangement of metallic ammunition production was under way by the autumn of 1938'. Neville Chamberlain had been involved with the Kynoch Works when he was in business and the official history of the factory stresses that 'we can take a melancholy pride in the fact that a year's delay was won by a former colleague'. Because of this 'the whole great machine, freshly serviced and already tested in low gear, was ready to spring into full and pulsing life'.

At its peak, 20,000 people grafted at Kynoch's. Others were employed at works in Kings Norton, Plume

King George VI inspecting cartridge cases, probably at Kynoch's in Witton, 27 October 1939.

Street, Aston, and Selly Oak - where the employees sent out 'large quantities of shoe rivet wire used in making boots for the Russian army'. But the main product of Kynoch's was 'a remarkable variety of small arms ammunition, from 20mm cartridges to large Q.F. cases, from detonators to anti-tank devices'. Senior staff who were experts on metals were also involved deeply in the Tube Alloys Project, the code name for the United Kingdom's Atomic Energy effort. (*Under Five Flags. The Story of the Kynoch Works, Witton, Birmingham, 1862-1962*, Birmingham, 1962, pp. 79-80). Two scientists from The University of Birmingham were prominent in the development of the atomic bomb itself. They were M.L.E. Oliphant, an Australian who was Poynting Professor of Physics, and Rudolf Peierls, a German who was Professor of Applied Mathematics. ('Who's Who in Team of Scientists', *Birmingham Post*, 7 August 1945).

As the city of a thousand trades and with skilled and adaptable workers, a host of Birmingham firms switched swiftly and successfully to war work. Craftsmen in the jewellery trade manufactured tools, parts and intricate components for large firms, whilst at the Sigma in Cumberland Street women such as Dorothy Teece shifted from the manufacture of electrical conduit fittings to the production of landmines. British Timken Ltd of Cheston Road, Aston, manufacturers of ball and roller bearings, produced the bearings for 'Operation Pluto' - a pipeline under the English Channel which supplied the Allies with oil after D-Day. Nearby at the Hercules Cycle Company, Rocky Lane, workers turned out bicycles for the armed services - as they did at the James Cycle Company in Tyseley. Military motorcycles were produced both at the Norton in Bracebridge Street, Aston and at the Ariel in Grange Road, Bournbrook, whilst the wheels for them were made by women at places such as the Midland Wheel, Avenue Road, Aston. (*Arms and the Jeweller*, Birmingham, 1946; Dorothy Teece, Letter, July 1996; '"Operation Pluto"', *Birmingham Post*, 26 May 1945).

GB 842 b c
(3. Ang.)
Nur für den Dienstgebrauch
Bild Nr. 1051b-454 (v) Lfl. 3
Aufnahme vom 27. 11. 40

Birmingham

Werk für elektrische Maschinen u. Akkumulatoren

Länge (westl. Greenw.): 1° 54′ 25″ Breite: 52° 29′ 30″
Mißweisung: — 11° 20′ (Mitte 1941) Zielhöhe über NN 122 m

Maßstab etwa 1 : 4 300

Genst. 5. Abt. Dezember 1941

Karte 1 : 100 000
GB/E 23

1. Verwaltungsgebäude, massiv, mehrstöckig, versch. Dacharten etwa 4 000 qm
2. Fabrikationsgebäude, massiv, mehrstöckig, versch. Dacharten etwa 9 000 qm
3. Presserei und Stanzerei, massiv, mehrstöckig, versch.
5. Graugießerei, massiv, versch. Dacharten etwa 600 qm
6. Kartonagenfabrik, massiv, versch. Dacharten etwa 5 000 qm
7. Fabrikationsgeb. und Reparaturwerkstätten etwa 4 800 qm
8. Überdachter Laufgang über die Straße

A German aerial photograph, targeting a Birmingham electrical machinery and battery factory, perhaps Lucas Ltd, Hockley, 27 November 1940. The photo includes descriptions of the buildings, their roof types, their heights and their functions.

In Brearley Street, Summer Lane, the hooks and eyes firm of Newey Brothers sent out clothing fasteners for the military as well as shell cases for the Bofors anti-aircraft guns; and in Barr Street, Hockley J. Hudson and Company supplied whistles to the Royal Navy, the Army, the Royal Air Force, the Merchant Navy and Civil Defence. Down the road in Great Hampton Street, Canning's re-polished shells and manufactured dynamos for degaussing. This device neutralised the magnetism of ship's hulls and gave them safety from mines. Across the city in Leopold Street, Highgate, the brass bedstead business of Samuel Heath's made blow lamps, paraffin stoves, firing pins and primers; whilst Docker's of Rotton Park Street, Ladywood devised camouflage paint. Even the chocolate maker Cadbury's moved into war work. A subsidiary company, Bournville Utilities, employed 2,000 people who made machine tools, lathes, milling machines, aero parts, anti-aircraft rockets and respirators. (*Newey. One hundred and seventy-five years of progress*, Birmingham, no date, p. 11; J. Hudson & Co., *Eighty Years Sound Development*, Birmingham, 1950, p. 18; David A. Thomas, *The Canning Story. 1785-1985*, London, 1985, pp. 104-5, thanks to Roger Martin; *100 Years on Samuel Heath & Sons PLC*, Birmingham, 1990, p. 3; *Cadbury at Bournville*, Birmingham, no date, p. 24, thanks to Ken Wright).

Sandbagging the Town Hall to protect it from bombing, September 1939.

By 1944, 400,000 Brummies were involved in war work. This was a greater percentage of the population than in any other town or city in the United Kingdom. The importance of these munitions workers was matched by that of others in the war economy, such as Irene Wells of Bartley Green who was one of thousands of women in the Land Army. They played a major role in growing food and by 1944 Warwickshire was producing all of Birmingham's flour, potatoes and milk. (Irene Wells, *My Life in the Land Army*, Alcester, 1991 edn). Railway workers were as significant, continuing to ensure the movement of goods. Each day the two main reception yards of the London

Midland and Scottish Railway dealt with between 6,000 and 7,000 wagons holding coal. ('Soldiers of the Line', *Birmingham Mail*, 20 September 1941). Similar movement was evident on the Great Western Line, for which John Busby worked. When war broke out he was a seventeen-year old porter at Snow Hill Station. He was registered as in a reserved occupation and was directed to train as a signalman. His 'crash course' instructor was Arthur Round, who 'taught me well & luckily I took to it & learned it very quickly'. The most important advice he was given was 'never to panic & never desert your box'. He heeded these instructions in November 1940. Before he went to work an incendiary landed in his family's garden in Heybarnes Road, Small Heath. John helped to put this out and whilst the raid continued he set off for the station. In the pitch dark he rode his bike into a bomb crater. Lying there dazed, a policeman told him he was sitting on a delayed action bomb. Pulled out of the crater, John resumed his journey, carrying his bent and battered bike. When he arrived at work, the station was 'in a right mess, it had sustained several hits, with bombs & incendiaries, glass from the roof was everywhere'. Undaunted, John went to do his job in the North Signal Box.' (Letter, February 1995).

Other railway workers were as conscientious and resolute. Peter Frederick Smout, an engine cleaner, was awarded the George Medal for his valour when he drove his engine to 'a blazing goods yard and drew wagons to safety while bombs were falling'. He did this three times, even though 'the off-side of the footplate was too hot to touch'. His colleague, Frederick Francis Blake, was honoured similarly. An examiner, he 'propelled a burning wagon to safety by hand, removed other trucks, and acted as a shunter to Smout, operating the point levers which had become very hot'. They were supervised by James Ernest Clarke, yard master's clerk at Bordesley Junction, who was given the British Empire Medal. ('Raid Heroes', *Birmingham Mail*, 25 January 1941).

CHAPTER THREE

BRUM BATTERED BUT NOT DEFEATED:
THE BLITZ

A Brummie survivor injured when an oil bomb fell at the door of his Anderson Shelter in Slade Road, Erdington, 20 October 1940. Another seven people were also saved by the shelter.

Burnt but not Broken: August-September 1940

By early July 1940 Hitler had realised that the United Kingdom was not going to sue for peace and he issued Directive No.16 'on preparations for a landing operation in England'. Code-named 'Sea Lion' it was unfeasible because the German Navy was weaker than the Royal Navy. It could work only if the *Luftwaffe* controlled the skies and was able to bomb British ships. To achieve this mastery the Royal Air Force had to be defeated by mid-September, before the more turbulent autumn weather made it impossible for German planes to protect the invasion fleet. On 1 August 1940 Hitler put out another directive ordering the establishment of 'conditions favourable to the conquest of Britain' and demanding an 'intensification of the air war'. This started on 'The Day of the Eagle', 13 August, and the Battle of Britain was begun.

The Germans aimed to destroy the R.A.F. They focused on attacking British airfields, on factories making anti-aircraft weapons and on ports on the south coast. Throughout the rest of August and early September fierce air battles raged by day over the south of England. Both the R.A.F. and the *Luftwaffe* suffered heavy losses but in a bloody conflict the British emerged victorious. On 7 September the Germans launched a massive raid with 300 bombers aiming for the docks of London. Intelligence reports suggested that this was part of the build-up to invasion and at 8.07 that evening the code word 'Cromwell' was sent out to military units throughout the United Kingdom. Everywhere church bells rang out in warning - but there was no movement of German ships towards Britain. On 15 September the R.A.F. defeated the *Luftwaffe* in another huge fight in the skies, and two days later Hitler postponed his invasion plans 'until further notice'. But if the invasion was put off, then the blasting of British cities continued in darkness when the R.A.F. was unable to attack the enemy.

The historian A.J.P. Taylor has argued that 'the German bomber offensive at night against Great Britain grew more or less accidentally out of the Battle of Britain and was continued as much in retaliation for British bombing as for any other reason'. He also believed that the *Luftwaffe's* raid on the capital on 7 September began the indiscriminate bombing of British cities that was 'to continue throughout the war'.

The wreckage of a German plane in a back garden somewhere in Birmingham.

(A.J.P. Taylor, *The Second World War. An illustrated history*, London, 1975, pp. 69-70 and 72.). The evidence does not support his assertions. First, there was no accident about the German air raids on the great towns and cities of the United Kingdom. Their aim was to demoralise the civilian population and to disrupt war work in factories. Second, the *Luftwaffe's* attacks were not in retaliation for British bombing on German cities. Dover had been hit as early as 25 May 1940, and raids soon followed on Folkestone, Portsmouth, Plymouth, Liverpool, Birmingham and elsewhere. Ostensibly, the Germans focused on 'legitimate' targets, but they also killed many civilians. By contrast, the R.A.F. concentrated on military installations in its bombing on Germany. Not until 25 August was Berlin raided and that was in reprisal for an assault on London the previous day. On this occasion German planes had missed their target of aircraft factories in Kingston-on-Thames and mistakenly had dropped their bombs on the capital. Third, the *Luftwaffe's* raid of 7 September on London did not signal the indiscriminate bombing of British cities. Like Liverpool, Birmingham was attacked regularly from early August 1940, and the German planes did not target munitions factories only.

There is some debate over the date of the first raid on the city. Theresa Bothwell believes that bombs were dropped in Erdington on the day that war was declared.

She remembered that her family went to an early mass and after hearing Chamberlain's broadcast she and her sister went upstairs to change into their play dresses. As they did so 'we heard a plane flying overhead'. Dashing to the window they saw it pass by their road in Birches Green and 'almost immediately we heard Thump, Thump, Thump'. Later that day they went to Rookery Park where 'there was a circle of people looking down at the ground'. Their attention was fixed on two small craters, and nearby was a similar hole in the ground. (Peter Leather, 'Hidden City', *Metronews*, 14 March 1996).

No official records corroborate this account, but they do confirm that a lone German pilot bombed Erdington on 9 August 1940. Edwin E. Wilkes was woken by the sound of the enemy plane going over his home in Goosemoor Lane. He realised that it was not from the nearby Castle Bromwich aerodrome because 'it was not droning high in the sky, offering itself for searchlight practice. It was travelling low and fast, with a sound different to any I had heard before.' Soon after the engine petered out 'before opening up to a roar' and 'almost immediately came the sound of a crash, followed by a thud'. Alarmed, Edwin reached for his gas mask 'but the string of the sixpenny canister which contained it caught on the wooden bedpost and in my haste/panic I was unable to free it'. Going to the window, in the distance he saw 'two dull red glows' appearing to jump from low in the sky. They arched downwards and disappeared to be followed by two more flashes. (Letter, 11 April 1995).

Ethel Bishop was nearby in Montague Road:

> I was lying in bed when there was a terrific bang. God! I thought someone is having a bad thunderstorm - the next moment there was an even worse bang & the house shook. Oh no! I thought we have been hit by a thunderbolt. I went rushing downstairs but before I reached the bottom there was another bang. We put coats over our night clothes & opened the front door & found that two of the houses opposite were missing. We had the first bombs that dropped on Brum. The first fell on Lydford Grove, the second on Montague Rd & the third I think was Erdington Hall Rd. There were no sirens sounded that night. (Letter, 19 March 1995).

Air raid damage on the Tyburn Road, Erdington, 14 August 1940.

The Fry family lived in one of the houses destroyed in Montague Road. Neighbours sped to help when they heard the crash from the fall of the building. They battled through the rubble until the A.R.P. workers arrived. Mr and Mrs Fry were brought out safely, as were their two daughters. It took two hours to free their eighteen-year old son who was on leave from the army. All the ambulances which had raced to the spot had been used and so the injured teenager was put in a demolition vehicle. Tragically, Jimmy Fry died on the way to the General Hospital. He was the first of 2,241 Brummies to be killed in the Blitz on Birmingham. ('Houses Damaged', *Birmingham Mail*, 9 August 1940; Mrs Parry, Letter, August 1996; Jean and John Cox, Letter, 12 August, 1996).

There were a number of vital munitions works in and about Erdington and it is likely that the raider had been searching for one of them. On 13 August the *Luftwaffe* found one its main targets when it bombed the Castle Bromwich aircraft factory. Five workers were killed and two other Brummies died elsewhere in the city. Following this raid the Germans increasingly attacked working-class neighbourhoods, where many factories were cheek-by-jowl with housing. On 15 August the south side of the city was targeted 'when Hay Mills and Small Heath suffered the worst'. ('Seventy Air Attacks on Birmingham', *Birmingham Weekly Post*, 29 September 1944). Nearby in Bordesley Green a home-made shelter was hit. There were seven deaths - Mr and Mrs Wall, their daughter Dora, Mr Wall's 79 year old dad, and three friends. ('Midlands Raid', *Birmingham Mail*, 16 August 1940). The raids continued, as the diary of Glenys George records: '17th, 3½ hrs; 18th, 4 hrs; 19th, 3¼ hrs; 23rd, 2½ hrs; 24th, 7½ hrs ICI, Aston'. (Letter, 19 March 1995). On look out for the *Luftwaffe* were volunteers from the Royal Observer Corps. Based in 1,400 posts nationwide, they

Wrecked barges at the wharf of canal carriers Fellows, Morton and Clayton in Fazeley Street, Digbeth.

relayed information to Fighter Command and to A.R.P. headquarters. In turn the information was passed on to factories and schools where sirens were placed. During these early attacks there were complaints that air raid warnings did not sound early enough. Peter Donnelly remembered that 'there were no sirens, only policemen pedalling furiously on their bicycles up and down the road outside our home, blowing long piercing blasts on their whistles'. (Peter Donnelly, 'Memories on the 50th Anniversary of V.E. Day', unpublished manuscript, April 1995, p. 2).

Because of the lack of alert, sometimes people were unaware of German planes until the bombs dropped - a factor which perhaps led to the loss of lives on the night of 19 August. Bombs were dropped in 'a thickly-populated district' and 'house property in a working-class district suffered considerable damage and the streets were littered with glass'.

One of the houses demolished was in a row of four and was occupied by a family named Smith. Mrs Elizabeth Smith, the grandmother aged 65, who has been bedridden for two years was killed, and also her grand-daughter Joyce (aged 4). The little girl's parents were among the injured. The other house affected is 100 yards away on the other side of the road and in a row of 12. It was occupied by a family of which the father was at work at the time. Here two schoolboys were killed. There were two other members of the family at home, and both were injured. The mother, aged 42, received a fractured arm and cuts, and her daughter, Joyce, aged 16, severe lacerations to her body. She was taken to the hospital where she died.

('Widespread Raids', *Birmingham Mail*, 20 August 1940).

The anguish of the father when he came home from work cannot be imagined. Birmingham was not alone. People were grieving in cities across England and Wales. Such suffering, such deaths and such raids make A.J.P. Taylor's position untenable. German air raids were indiscriminate before the attack on London on 7 September.

It is generally accepted 'that the first major night attack on the United Kingdom' was on Liverpool on 28 August. (Edwin Webb and John Duncan, *Blitz Over Britain*, Tunbridge Wells, 1990, p.96). There is no doubt that Merseyside was affected severely by the Blitz, and except for London, more people were killed there than anywhere else in the United Kingdom. Like Birmingham, Liverpool is mentioned rarely in

Rescue workers at a Birmingham house where several people were killed when the building collapsed after a bomb hit it, 26 August 1940.

commentaries on the Second World War and nothing should detract from the heroism of Merseysiders. However, the first major night raid in the United Kingdom took place on 25 August when the city centre of Birmingham was attacked by 50 bombers. A high-explosive bomb and incendiaries hit the Market Hall, shattering its roof and burning it out. Completed in 1835, the building was impressive in its Greek-style architecture and was embedded in the affections of Brummies. Its basement was used as an air-raid shelter. Fortunately, the attack happened on a Sunday and no-one was in the Market Hall apart from the nightwatchman, Mr V. Leverington. Before 'he made for the adjacent shelter he unlocked the cages containing live creatures and released the stock, which made for the swing doors and so into the street'. He was awarded the R.S.P.C.A. silver medal for his courage.

Incendiaries destroyed property elsewhere in the city centre and in the suburbs. In one of them a witness watched as dust-laden smoke poured between the trees. Above, 'the sky was red from the many fires, an injured woman cried out of the uncertain distance, a dog howled, some men killed, and others rescued. The whole nightmare scene expressed the bottomless pit of inanity of life in Europe in the 20th Century.' ('One Wild Night', *Birmingham Mail*, 12 September 1940). Twenty-five people were killed in this raid, including Robert King, an A.F.S. worker, his wife Maude and their fourteen-month old baby, Robert. Amongst the survivors were Mr and Mrs Williams. A high-explosive shell landed two feet from their Anderson Shelter, waking their son Albert. The twelve-year old boy told reporters that his dad said, '"We're OK this time," so I just settled down to have another doze'. The Williams family stopped in the shelter for about another hour 'and then when it went quiet we climbed out and saw a great big hole at the back. I don't mind admitting it rather put the wind up me'. ('Market Wrecked', *Birmingham Mail*, 26 August 1940).

A few days later the sight of the Bull Ring was described by a member of the Mass Observation team:

> *The Market Hall was only a shell, only the walls were standing. Through the windows it was possible to see black, charred beams of wood, but the best view was obtained at the side through an opening in the wall. A barrier had been put up here, and a number of men and children were leaning on it. It was simply a mass of rubble, charred beams, pieces of iron, bricks and a few utensils: the iron frames of the stalls remained, and on one of them there was still the name plaque, 'Albert Pope' . . . two small Union Jacks had been bravely stuck into the wreckage, and a third was lying on the ground . . . further along the firm of Yates had chalked beside their new address, 'Burnt but not broke'.* ('Town and District Survey', *Mass Observation Archive*, 3 September 1940, cited in Phillada Ballard, editor, *A City at War. Birmingham 1939-1945*, Birmingham 1985, p. 27).

A major feature of the Market Hall had been a striking clock which fascinated Brummies and visitors. It had three bells, one of which was three hundredweight, which were struck by solid oak figures of three knights and a dame. They were burned to ashes. (Cutting from the *Birmingham Gazette* supplied by Frank Collins). After the war a defused 1,000 pound bomb was placed in the Market Hall. Nicknamed Satan, it was used as a collecting box for charity. (Brian Henderson, Letter, 30 June 1996).

On 26 August, the day after the Bull Ring was blitzed, the German High Command issued a communiqué. It announced that 'last night numerous planes flew over Birmingham, Kingston and Coventry, where aircraft factories and armament works were bombed. Violent explosions and fires were observed.' The Germans also admitted that 'some British planes, for the first time since the war, flew over Berlin and dropped several incendiary bombs on the outskirts of the city'. They charged the R.A.F. with attacking other places where 'non-military targets were indiscriminately bombed'. To the people of Birmingham and other British cities this accusation was full of hypocrisy. Since at least 16 August the *Luftwaffe* had been bombing civilian sites as much as industrial targets. The raid which burned the Market Hall emphasised this fact. ('Concentrated Raids', *Birmingham Mail*, 26 August 1940).

The Nazis named Birmingham as a place which had been bombed. The local newspapers did not. From the first attack Brum was referred to as a 'Midlands Town'. This treatment marked Birmingham out as most other British towns and cities were referred to specifically when they were bombed. On 26 August, for example, the *Birmingham Mail* reported that 'the air raids on Saturday night were widespread, and the places affected included the City of London, Portsmouth, Southsea, Ramsgate and the Midlands'. ('Saturday's Raids', *Birmingham Mail*, 26 August 1940). Anthony Sutcliffe and Roger Smith believed that the local press had a self-imposed censorship. Birmingham was not named 'for fear that the *Luftwaffe's* confidence in its navigational aids would be increased if it received confirmation that its aircraft had bombed the right city'. It is difficult to agree with this opinion. (Sutcliffe and Smith, *History of Birmingham*, pp. 25-6).

Birmingham newspapers usually did not name their city - although the *Birmingham Mail* did so occasionally, as on 28 August. ('Birmingham Blaze', *Birmingham Mail*, 28 August 1940). Yet their reports did suggest strongly that Brum had been bombed. This was obvious in two main ways. First, from statements such as the Midland town possessed a 'market hall erected more than 100 years ago, which was the resort of the people particularly of the weekend'. ('Market Wrecked', *Birmingham Mail*, 26 August 1940). And second, by

The burnt-out shell of the Market Hall, 27 August 1940.

the naming of people who were killed during raids or who had lucky escapes. Only a local newspaper could have such knowledge, indicating that the *Birmingham Mail*, *Birmingham Post*, *Evening Despatch* and *Birmingham Gazette* were describing attacks on their city. Moreover, after each raid information was given openly in notices hung in Margaret Street, at St Philip's Cathedral and other public places. These indicated the names and addresses of those people who were killed, injured or made homeless by raids. (Mary Foster, Letter, *April 1941. Evening Mail Special*, April 1981, p. 7).

There is another explanation for the fact that Brum was not mentioned specifically. The investigations of Marjorie Ashby have revealed that early in 1939 'the Government had declared, should there be a war, because of Birmingham's importance to the war industry, it was essential that the Germans should not have confirmation that the *Luftwaffe* had penetrated the defences around it'. (Letter, 21 January 1996). This interpretation seems to be supported by statements made during the war. On 12 October 1940 the editor of the *Birmingham Mail* reported a decision by the city's Markets and Fairs Committee to turn the Market Hall into an open-air market. His editorial went on:

> *From which it seems safe to assume that this modestly veritable Bull Ring landmark has lost its roof. It is not pertinent here to enquire how - we hope we know our duties in the interest of national defence - and we shall be content to leave it to public speculation whether it is a case of moths, the death-watch beetle or merely another hint of fresh air fiends in the Council House!* ('The Market Mystery', *Birmingham Mail*, 12 October 1940).

Four days later a communiqué was issued by the Air Ministry. It gives further support for the belief that the air raids on Birmingham were censored, unlike those on most other cities. The statement indicated that 'London and a town in the Midlands were the principal objectives of last night's raids'. ('Roads Closed in Midlands Town', *Birmingham Mail*, 16 October 1940).

The censorship on Birmingham caused upset locally, as it did in Hull which was usually described as 'a North-East Town' when it was attacked. Herbert Morrison was the war-time Home Secretary and in his memoirs he sympathised with the people of Humberside 'for having to endure such a cloak of anonymity during the war'. (Webb and Duncan, *Blitz Over Britain*, p. 132). Birmingham has never received such recognition. In December 1940 the editor of the *Birmingham Mail* reflected public opinion when he stated that the city had been 'raided well and truly on more than one night'. He went on to question 'why aren't we given specific details as to the damage which has been done?' The reason was simple, 'the experts, time and again have assured us that the publication of detailed particulars regarding air raid damage would be slipping a useful card into the enemy's hands'. Showing a disregard for the censors, the editor then recorded some of the places worst affected by the bombing on Brum. ('Scars of War', *Birmingham Mail*, 9 December, 1940).

The blitzing of the Bull Ring on 25 August was followed the next night by a six hour attack which hit the BSA Factory in Armoury Road. But as with all the *Luftwaffe* raids on 'military targets', bombs were dropped on the surrounding districts. There was devastation across Small Heath, Bordesley Green, Sparkbrook and Sparkhill. A survivor explained that 'as we lay in the shelter we heard the machine coming down as though it were a fast fighter. Then came the scream of the bomb, followed by the terrible crunch as it made contact with the buildings'. He had no doubt that the German pilot deliberately targeted 'what he must have known to have been private dwellings'. One family, the Fosters, had a 'remarkable story of the raid'. Fifty-five years later it was recalled by Beatrice Sherlock:

> *I was lodging at my future husband's sister, Mrs E. Foster 19, Cherrywood Road, Bordesley Green, B'ham. Her husband Joe dug a large hole in the small back garden to put the Anderson Shelter. On the Sunday night the Market Hall, Bull Ring was bombed. The next night a direct hit on our shelter. No-one badly injured, they dug me up from being blown upside down, the blast taking one stocking off leaving the shoe on and vice-versa on the other. After being carried to an underground shelter for the night we returned next morning not believing how we could have escaped.*

Beatrice was given clothes and shoes by relations at number 46. Then with Evelyn Foster she limped to the battered house where 'there was a policeman standing on the step'. Asking if she could go upstairs, the officer told her 'he could not stop me but had to warn that everything could collapse if I trod on stairs'. Just eighteen-years old, 'wanting to salvage my belongings and only 8st' Beatrice went to the bedroom while a crowd gathered. She remembered that the *Birmingham Mail* reported that 'Evelyn was annoyed with Joe putting in the shelter as the dirt came right up as far as the back door step. How glad I was he ignored the mess. It saved six lives that night.' (Letter, 21 March 1995; 'Midland Raids', *Birmingham Mail*, 27 August 1940).

Children in houses destroyed by explosives in Small Heath, 18 October 1940.

That raid of 26 August had begun a short time after midnight. At about 3.30 a.m. its focus shifted towards the city centre. Most affected was the Snow Hill area where 'fires in a huge quadrangle, bounded by Summer Row, Edmund Street, Livery Street and St Paul's Square were in danger of joining up into a single conflagration'. Warehouses, factories and shops were alight 'and the roadway itself had melted, with the "liquid fire" running along to set more buildings alight'. A.F.S trailer pumps were pulled into the district by 'every imaginable vehicle from old taxis to Rolls Royces'. In all 90 crews were involved in fighting the blazes. One of them was in Newhall Street which was 'nearly all alight'. The officer in charge positioned his hoses and 'left the jets to their own devices'. Noticing a serious fire close to Snow Hill he went to investigate 'but could see only a sea of flames with apparently no limit'. To get a better view of the situation, one of the men was sent up the turntable ladder 'but a sudden change of wind engulfed him in flames and when we brought him down he had received very serious burns to the face and hands'. By now the firemen 'had almost reached the end of their strength'. Worn out, they had inadequate water supplies, their communications were disrupted and a central control system was not working effectively. A call for assistance was sent out to other brigades in the region and support came from the Black Country, Sutton Coldfield, Coventry, Lichfield and Tamworth. By 5.30 a.m. all the fires were under control, and the succeeding hours were spent damping down, turning over the ruins, making up hoses and re-equipping and repairing appliances. (Klopper, *The Fight Against Fire*, pp. 85-6).

According to Sutcliffe and Smith, after the attack on 26 August 'this first series of raids petered out'. (Sutcliffe and Smith, *Birmingham 1939-70*, p. 26). The Luftwaffe's attacks may have lessened in intensity but there was no real respite until the middle of September. The diary of Glenys George indicates that there were raids on Birmingham nightly from 27 August to 7 September. After one night's rest, bombing resumed on 9 September and went on for the next three nights. This was followed by another short lull and more raids until 16 September. (Letter, 18 March 1995). None of these attacks lasted for less than two hours, the majority went on for over five hours and one continued for nine hours. All of them damaged houses and other property, including the C & A Stores in Corporation Street and the tramlines on the Tyburn Road in Pype Hayes. All of them led to injuries and in some of them lives were lost. One of the dead was an England schoolboy football international.

A police officer shepherding a crowd away from a pub bombed in the Newtown Row neighbourhood, 17 October 1940.

He was out with his dad when the raid began on 28 August and he 'ran home to be by his mother's side'. When he reached the house his mom was out 'and he had barely got inside when he was killed on the spot'. On another occasion six people were killed when their Anderson Shelter took a direct hit. They included three-year old Peter Bradley and his mom and dad. ('Birmingham Blaze', *Birmingham Mail*, 28 August 1940; 'Midland Raid', *Birmingham Mail*, 29 August 1940; 'Shelter Hit', *Birmingham Post*, 3 September 1940; 'Raids on Midlands', *Birmingham Mail*, 3 September 1940)

Unlike the other local newspapers, the editor of the *Birmingham Mail* occasionally ignored the directives of the Government and named his city in reports of raids. On 6 September one of his headlines proclaimed 'Not daunted. Birmingham's Fine Morale. Standing Up To Raids. Work Goes On As Usual.' A week later Brummies endured the longest raid of the war so far, whilst on 16 September a German bomber collided with the cable of a barrage balloon and crashed to the ground. Three of the crew were killed and two were captured. ('All-Night Raids', *Birmingham Mail*, 13 September 1940;

'Bomber's Fate', *Birmingham Mail*, 17 September 1940). **Over the next few weeks enemy attacks lessened, although on 27 September Fort Dunlop was attacked in daylight. Miss B.J. Wright was a junior clerk at the works. With the other employees she left the premises at 5.30 p.m. to catch her bus home and 'as we stood in queues a German plane dived out of the clouds (no warnings) and opened fire with a machine gun. He was so low we could see him laughing in the cock pit. It was pouring with rain and we all dived for the gutters flat on our faces.'** (Letter, 15 February 1995; 'Midland Town Bombed', *Birmingham Post*, 28 September 1940).

This was not an isolated incident. Bill Drew lived and worked in Aston and 'one morning a colleague arrived pale and shaken and late for work'. He told his mates that he had been on a Midland Red Bus 'which had been attacked and machine gunned by a low flying German plane'. Fortunately there were no casualties and 'we assured him he had a good excuse for being late'. (Letter, 1996). Mr W.H. James went through the same ordeal. As a child he lived in Francis Street, Ashted. During one night raid he and his older sister were on the way to shelter in a neighbour's cellar:

when we became trapped in an entry by German Planes machine gunning everywhere. My sister told me to lie flat on the ground which I did otherwise I may not have been here today. The person whose cellar we went to was an old gentleman who would stand in his backyard swearing and waving his stick at the German Planes overhead. It was a wonder he never got killed as he would not take cover in the shelter. My father during one Air-Raid fell down the steps just as a bomb exploded somewhere and everybody laughed at him, he even laughed himself over it. (Letter, April, 1995).

George Woods was only a baby at the start of the war. When his family was bombed out of 8, Sycamore Terrace, Wolseley Street, Bordesley they moved a few doors down. Soon after they were sheltering nearby in the basement of Carr's Paints in Artillery Street and the factory was bombed. Everyone 'had to do a quick exit as fire soon spread

A.R.P. workers at badly-damaged houses in Bromford Lane, Erdington, 24 August 1940.

through the building'. Seeking 'some safe place mom, with me in her arms and an older sister and brother on her apron strings went into the park in Garrison Lane where she and other women were strafed from German planes'. (Letter, 26 May 1995).

The raid of 27 September brought to an end the first stage of the Blitz on the city. It is regarded by some historians as a period when the bombing was light. It was not to those who went through it. During August and September 1940 over 100 Brummies were killed, hundreds more were injured, and the emotions of thousands of survivors were haunted and harried. As one of them put it, the noise of the bombing 'sounded as if the world had come to an end'. ('Raids on Midlands', *Birmingham Mail*, 3 September 1939). Hilda Mleczko, then Hilda Tipper, had similar feelings. Living in Colonial Road, Bordesley Green, 'the war, to me was one long string of fear-filled nights in places where you laughed and joked to keep your spirits up. In between were surprisingly happy times, a concert or a Vera Lynn song, like a message from heaven. And there were those blessedly quiet spells in the bombing lulls, when you slept a sort of desperate sleep.' (Hilda Mleczko, *My Book of Memories. Picking Up the Pieces*, Glace Bay, Canada, no date, p. 22). Whether or not the attacks of the *Luftwaffe* caused much damage the nightly air-raid warnings had a harrowing effect on people, as was emphasised by Violet Hoare:

> *You expected it; you waited for it; you knew it was going to happen yet it never failed to make your heart jump into your throat, your mouth run dry and that familiar feeling of panic overwhelm you when that first whining note of the fluctuating wail that was the air raid siren heralded another night in the air raid shelter listening to the bombs find their target, and where we lived, in Nechells, there were plenty of prime targets. We were surrounded by gas works, railway goods yards and factories involved in war work.* (Letter, 20 February 1995).

Though Our Houses Are Down Our Spirits Are Up: October 1940

On 14 October Clementine Churchill, the wife of the Prime Minister, visited Birmingham. She went to two factories and to one neighbourhood which had been damaged by bombing. One of the local women placed a Union Jack on a pile of tiles and Mrs Churchill then spoke to Mr and Mrs Hartle whose house was in ruins. They told her 'our house is down, but our spirits are still up'. The reporter added that 'the demonstration of unflinching courage in this typical working-class suburban district was the same everywhere'. ('Raid Damage', *Birmingham Mail*, 14 October 1940). That evening the resolve of the people was tested yet again when German attacks on Birmingham resumed in earnest. Amongst those killed were a number of women in 'a hostel for aged women'. ('Midland Raid', *Birmingham Mail*, 15 October 1940).

The next night, 15 October, 59 people were killed in more severe attacks. The Germans dropped over one hundred high explosive bombs, several delayed action bombs and hundreds of incendiaries. Rowton House was hit as was a home for the elderly, although none of the 250 women were hurt. Nor were any of the 95 people who were sheltering in the basement of the Jewish school in St Luke's Road, off Bristol Street, where a bomb came through the ceiling. Nearby a disabled teenager, Jack Haden, saw an incendiary fall on the roof of a church. He and a twelve-year old boy climbed 70 feet up the spouting and 'kicked the bomb through the slates and before it could fire the wooden rafters it fell directly in the centre aisle'. Only a few chairs were burned. ('Crippled Hero', *Birmingham Mail*, 16 October 1940).

Over the next week the Luftwaffe kept up the pressure. By now Brummies were becoming accustomed to a new way of life forced on them by the Blitz, as Mr R.S. Timmins stressed:

'Quick, get to bed and grab a wink of sleep - are your clothes all ready? - shoes, trousers, jumper, coat. Don't touch that candle!' This was our mother repeating the routine every night through the bombing years. We lived in Saltley. Mom worked in a factory. Dad was in the army and our family of six shared an Anderson Shelter with neighbours. Although quite roomy it was also very crowded and the reason why we tried to get a little sleep before a raid. As expected the dreaded sirens started to wail. Another frightening night of bombing and wondering if we would still have a house at the end of it.

Houses obliterated in the Newtown Row area, 17 October 1940.

One night the youngster went through the usual procedures but by the time he reached the shelter he realised he felt extremely cold in the lower region. Half asleep and in his haste to dress himself 'I had put my legs through the bottom of my jumper and into the arms, pulling up what I thought were my trousers, the open neck end exposing where my underpants should have been - and weren't we in a crowded shelter. This was an embarrassment but we've laughed many times about it.' (Letter, 27 February 1995).

In the midst of fear and consternation there were many humorous incidents. Margaret Newell's family used a neighbour's shelter and during one raid her pregnant mother had a craving for pickled onions which 'had got the better of her'. Dashing across the road to her home an air raid warden shouted at her to stop. Asking who she was, she told him her name and the reason why she was on the street. The retort was terse, 'Blow the pickled onions, there's a bloody air raid on. Get back inside Millie!'

(Letter, 22 February 1995). Elsie Wood also ventured outside during an attack. She lived at 3 back of 53, Clifford Street, Lozells and one night her son remembered that:

> *a bomb dropped on Mrs Morris's house across the street. Our Dad and I were fire-watching and it blew us up the entry. Luckily we were ok, just covered in muck. When the dust settled we looked up the street and there was Our Dear Old Mom with her washing basket picking up our poor neighbour's washing in the horse road, that had been blown off. Our Dad shouted, 'What yo doin ya silly bugga! Them Germans are machine gunning ya! Yo will get killed!' She just carried on shouting back, 'Shurrup yer face!' Elsie Wood was not bothered about Fatty Goering's Luftwaffe. No sir.* (Stan H. Wood, Letter, 21 February 1995).

Margaret Smith lived opposite a small grocer's shop owned by her dad, Sam Boswell, and his sister, Nell Tucker. One night there was 'a direct hit on a shop two doors away, known as Dawson's bacon and cooked meat'. Fortunately, no-one was killed, but the blast wrecked both the home and business of the Boswells. The next morning Margaret and her relatives went to look at the damage 'and my cousin turned to my sister (they were about 5 yrs old) & said "Well Nan can't give us some rocks & say ere yar ya greedy buggers now goo and play"'. (Letter, 23 June 1996). Laughter and bravery were matched by camaraderie. In 1940 Kenneth F. Street's dad was killed and his widow was left to bring up four children under six in the horrors and difficulties of the war. Living in Nelson Road, Witton, she was helped by 'a great family up the road called the Hickmans'. When the sirens sounded Kenneth and his brothers and sisters were 'frightened to death' but their kindly neighbours 'were down in a flash to carry us to the Anderson Shelter in their back garden. We did have our own shelter, but this family would not leave us alone.' (Letter, 20 February 1995).

Such support became increasingly important during the autumn of 1940. On 24 October the 'city's firefighters were again in great difficulties'. Shortly after midnight 189 major fires were blazing. (Klopper, *The Fight Against Fire*, p. 86). There were deaths and damage across the city centre. A shelter in Cox Street, Hockley was hit and 25 people were killed. The Empire Theatre was burned out, whilst the Hippodrome was saved from destruction by 'the diligence and courage of a handful of members of the male staff who smothered the incendiary bombs before they could get a hold on the roof'. Next door, Tony's Ballroom 'burned fiercely'. ('Scars of War', *Birmingham Mail*, 9 December 1940). Early in the morning of 25 October Mr G.J. Ball caught the 5 a.m. tram to town, on his way to work at the B.S.A. plant in Redditch. Alighting at Martineau Street, he walked to New Street.

> *In the middle of the road where there had been an island was a crater with a gas main still burning fiercely. To the left just inside New Street, Marshall and Snelgrove (posh) shop was wrecked by bombs and twisted black girders were hanging out of the road. I walked through the station to catch a Midland Red bus to Redditch in Bromsgrove Street. Nothing remained of one end of the street, where once had been a kosher butcher and the outfitters 'Sword and Robb' Ltd, were just ruins.* (Letter 24. February. 95).

That evening the 'Carlton' Picture House in Sparkbrook was bombed. The manager had told the customers to sit in the stalls beneath the balcony of the circle. This gave some protection but despite this precaution nineteen people were killed. Most of them were sitting in the rows nearest to the screen. ('Cinema Bombed', *Birmingham Mail*, 26 October 1940). One of the dead was a young Irishman, Ted Byrne, whose family had come to Birmingham just before the war. His dad had been in the British Army and later his brothers fought against the Nazis. The day of his killing remains imprinted on the mind of his little sister, Maggie Hughes:

> *He says to me this Friday night, he says, 'Mag, will you take them beer bottles over to the Antelope?' So I says, 'What for?' He says, 'I want to go to the pictures.' So I took them over to the Antelope, the beer bottles, got the money back and he says, 'When you get the money buy me five woodbines.' Anyway I bought him the five woodbines in Dunne's next door to the Antelope, came over and they were looking in the papers which pictures to go to and of course Ted, me brother, says, 'Oh, I've seen that one on the Carlton', he says, 'Typhoon', he says, 'I don't want to sit through a picture again.' So anyway they looked all at the Olympia, and the Warwick and all the other, 'Ah, there's nothing any good'. So this Richard Hannon and Nipper Bourke as they called him then . . . Jimmy Bourke, they says, 'Ah come on, go down the Carlton, it doesn't matter whether you've seen it again or not.' So anyway they went and that was the night that the Carlton got hit. And me Daddy was in the Home Guard then and they came up for him to go down and help take the bodies out. While me Daddy was down at the Carlton a copper come to the door and he says, 'Mrs Byrne?' . . . So she says, 'Yeh' He says, 'Well, would you go to Selly Oak Hospital as Edward has been brought there' . . . So when me Daddy came back with me brother-in-law John Devine, he, me Mammy says, 'You better go to Selly Oak. Ted. Ted's in there.' So he went in to Selly Oak. The nurse brought him to the ward, and he went in and he just, he seen Ted there and he says, 'Y'alright Ted?' He opened up his eyes and he says, 'Yes Dad' and then he died. He was only fifteen.*
> (Carl Chinn, 'Brummies', *BBC Radio WM*, 26 December, 1995).

The Carlton Picture House, Sparkbrook the day after it was hit by enemy planes, 26 October 1940.

There were numerous casualties amongst other Brummies on the night of 25 October and there were many heroes and heroines. One of them was Ivy Gilbert who put out incendiaries which fell in her street, modestly stating 'it was nothing'. Another was Arthur Bryant. He was the nightwatchman at the Lansdown Laundry in Studley Street, Sparkbrook where there were three shelters. As the raid began he directed about 50 women and children to safety. He was watching the last mother and baby go into a shelter when a fire bomb hit one end of the laundry. The blast threw him down the stairs and 'when I recovered my senses I saw the place was beginning to burn'. He and a friend 'got out most of the people from the shelters, for it was getting too hot for them' and took them to a nearby school. Returning to the laundry the men led out the horses from the stable, even though 'the place was going well now', and Arthur drove three of firm's vans away from blaze. Then he telephoned the fire service and helped fight the blaze and save the rear of the laundry itself. ('Raid Gallantry', *Birmingham Mail*, 26 October 1940).

Clearing up the debris at the first-aid post in Kent Street Baths, blasted by a high explosive bomb the previous night, 28 October 1940.

The *Luftwaffe* returned the next night. Ernest Price was an ambulanceman who noted the alerts sounded in Birmingham and some of the damage caused. His diary was dedicated 'to nights spent in the air-raid shelters (only at 1st) and dashing with the ambulance through burning, bomb-blasted streets conveying human "salvage" to hospital, of waiting in the garage, ambulance HQs and home for the bomb that seemed to be screaming down for your particular destruction'. For 26 October his entry reads: 'Clear Night. Night of Hell. Helped to remove injured from basement of Kent St Baths. Many killed. Took No of casualties to Selly Oak'. In Barker Street,

Summer Hill, fifteen people lost their lives when a shelter was bombed, and the raid caused serious fires in Constitution Hill and Holloway Head. By midnight 276 separate blazes were raging in the city. Eventually they were brought under control. ('How Birmingham Was Battered in the Blitz', *Birmingham Post Supplement*, 8 May 1945).

For three nights firefighters and other A.R.P. volunteers had combated the ravages of the *Luftwaffe*. They did so after going to work in the daytime. And for three weeks from 26 October alerts were sounded each night. Bombs were not dropped on every occasion but the nerves of Brummies were hammered by the daily strain and by the sight of so many burned-out or battered buildings. These included the Art Gallery, which was visited one Saturday morning by Elizabeth M. Horton and her mother. They were met by a friend, Donald Payler, who was a curator at the Museum. He took them inside the bruised premises.

I shall never forget the dust and debris at the top of the main staircase, and along the bridge. I remember climbing over a fallen pillar, and gazing up at the sky through a hole in the ceiling. We clambered on into one of the Natural History galleries (they were Mr Payler's special province). The wartime sense of humour was something that developed as a balm to our wounded feelings, and Donald Payler had it in good measure. He pointed at a stuffed moose: 'That old thing is really uninteresting, badly mounted and takes up too much space. If only Gerry could have dropped one on him . . .' A few days later Donald announced that 'Gerry' had paid

Stepping around the rubble in Smallbrook Street, the day after a bomb had struck the Empire Theatre in nearby Hurst Street, 25 October 1940.

the Gallery a return visit and had indeed landed an incendiary bomb on the moose's case. Mother was duly congratulatory, but was cut short: 'It fell on top of him, slid under his belly, singed two whiskers and fizzled out.' (Letter 18 February 1995).

The Town Hall also was hit, as was the Bristol Street Methodist Church. On 28 October it 'suffered severely' when seven incendiary bombs 'set fire to the roof, burning out the centre of it completely and leaving huge, gaping rents and charred timbers'. Bravely the clergyman, his wife and passers-by saved the tapestries and vestments. ('Many Fire Bombs', *Birmingham Mail*, 29 October 1940). The same night Birmingham Cathedral was damaged extensively. Alert to the possibility of damage, the authorities had removed the valuable stained glass windows of Sir Edward Burne-Jones and put them in safe storage.

Norman Bailey lived in Brookfields and on one of those fearful October nights 'we heard the bombers overhead and the sounds of explosions'. Seeing fires in the city centre and having an inquisitive nature 'I ran to the top of Camden Street where I knew I could see things better'. Further up that long street and towards Summer Hill, Bulpitt's factory was ablaze after taking a hit from an aerial torpedo. Looking up into a 'very bright moonlight night', Norman saw a bomber 'and ran home as fast as my little legs could carry me'. The next night his family sheltered in a church near Spring Hill, believing that 'they wouldn't bomb a church, would they?' Then the bombs began to drop and the thump-thump of explosions was heard. One of them was lower than the rest 'and the ground and building shook'. The lights went out in the shelter and people began shouting and screaming. After a few minutes the emergency lighting came on everyone 'was clasping each other, crying and sobbing into each other's arms.' When the all-clear came, Norman and his sister, Lily, went outside and saw a huge crater in the Dudley Road. ('Norman's Story', *Old Brum at War. Evening Mail Special*, 17 May 1993, p. 12).

Scenes of Destruction: November 1940

On 15 November Neville Chamberlain was cremated in London and a memorial service was held for him in St Martin's, the parish church of Birmingham. Many Britons saw Chamberlain as a weak man who capitulated to the aggression of Hitler. Large numbers of Brummies regarded him more positively. He was praised by the Lord Mayor, Alderman Wilfred Martineau, as one of the city's 'most distinguished sons' and as a man who 'had a passionate desire for the betterment of the health and living conditions of the people'. Dr Barnes, the Bishop of Birmingham, emphasised Chamberlain's 'brief but valiant effort for peace', adding movingly that though he did not succeed he 'failed greatly'. Support for the man who was a Freeman of the city and who founded the Municipal Bank was as obvious in the *Birmingham Weekly Post*. Its editor stressed that Chamberlain's 'supreme effort for peace' at Munich had been 'acclaimed by the whole nation, and not least by those who have since, in the light of events, been bitterest in the denunciation of the man who instigated it'. Crucially, he had bought the nation 'twelve months' reprieve, during which the United Kingdom became 'better prepared to wage war'. Sir Winston Churchill himself emphasised his predecessor's 'perfect sincerity' and his striving 'to save the world from the awful, devastating struggle in which we are now engaged'. Neville Chamberlain had resigned from the Government a month before his death. He refused all honours. He lived and died a simple citizen. In a world dominated by wicked men, Neville Chamberlain was a virtuous man. ('Neville Chamberlain', 'Memorial Service', and 'Premier's Tribute', *Birmingham Weekly Post*, 15 November, 1940).

PREMIER FACES HIS CRITICS

Mr. Chamberlain leaving Downing Street for Westminster yesterday.

Prime Minister Neville Chamberlain, 8 May 1940.

The night before the late premier's cremation, the contrast between evil and good was drawn clearly when the *Luftwaffe* attacked Coventry so heavily that a new word entered the German language - *Koventrieren*, Coventration. Its meaning was vile. It signified the razing to the ground of a place. Guided by radio beams and aided by a clear night and a full moon, German planes mercilessly pounded the centre of Coventry. Norman Burgess was in the A.F.S. and as he and his crew 'came down the Radford Rd to the top of Bishop St it looked as if the whole of Broadgate was alight'. (Letter, 1995). Firefighters like George Buffery were called in from as far away as Worcester. He told his daughter of how 'the Coventry born firemen were crying for the city they loved'. Yet amidst this 'hell on earth was the Salvation Army with a tea urn, my dad said they were so very brave because everybody was in the Anderson Shelters only the firemen and police fighting the fire'. (Margaret Buffery, Letter, 15 February, 1995).

Within a square mile, 80% of buildings were destroyed and 568 people were killed. Nine days later, the same fate befell Southampton - and later in the war Portsmouth, Plymouth and Hull suffered in similar ways. On 16 November the *Birmingham Gazette* proclaimed 'Coventry - Our Guernica'. Five days later the Germans were announcing that they had 'plastered Birmingham, the centre of the British armament and supply industries, with bombs'. According to the enemy High Command, 'in a succession of attacks hundreds of bomber planes discharged more than 500,000 kilogrammes of bombs (nearly 450 tons), some of the heaviest calibre'. Fires and explosions were 'visible at a great distance' and they 'were even more widespread than those in the raid on Coventry'. ('450 tons of bombs on Birmingham', *Birmingham Post*, 21 November 1940).

This horrific raid began at 7.17 p.m. on Tuesday 19 November when the first of 350 planes dropped flares and incendiaries, lighting up their targets for the heavy bombers to drop their slivers of death. Ten minutes later Fisher and Ludlow's was hit and from Birmingham's Control Centre teleprinter messages sped almost minute by minute to the Ministry of Home Security in London. Abruptly they told of the severity of the bombing on Brum:

> *21.35: Raid continues to be heavy and widespread. Fire position getting worse.*

> *22.34: New Street Station signal box, direct hit, station closed.*

> *22.50: Chance Bros, Smethwick; Wilmot Breeden, Tyseley; hit.*

> *22.55: Nine factories hit including BSA Small Heath, ICI Kynoch Works and Joseph Lucas.*

> *23.00: Some factory damage, mainly house property. Heavy raiding continues in some parts of the city.*

At 10.20 p.m. a high explosive fell at the rear of the 'Fountain' pub in Heath Mill Lane, Deritend shattering houses and trapping people in cellars. Eight people were killed and seventeen injured. Two minutes later the Prudential Buildings in Colmore Row were struck by a parachute landmine, damaging Boots, the Great Western Arcade, Grey's in Bull Street and the Bank of England in Temple Street. The raid ended finally at 4.30 a.m. Brum had been hammered for just over nine hours. (Celia Hall, 'Night of Horror', *November 1940. Evening Mail Special*, November 1980, p.3).

A Tyseley woman recorded her impressions of that terrible attack.

> *O God, what a night. 10¾ hours of anguish, misery, hunger and sleeplessness. 6.50 p.m. Tues. I had cooked a dinner and was about to serve it up when the sirens went. Les came and found Jacqueline and I sitting in the cubby hole. I said, 'I'll just dish the dinner up when the planes have slackened off for a moment'. They didn't slack off, they got worse, a terrific bombardment started, and then the house shook with bombs exploding. Les said, 'Dinner or no dinner, we're going down to the shelter. I hope you've bailed it out.' We scrambled into our clothes carried a blanket and cushions and hoped for the best. The sky was one blaze of light, gunfire was going on and did we run. We all got in safely, the floor was one large puddle, we sorted ourselves out and made the best of it, till a lull came. No lull came, as one wave of planes came over and was dying away so the next came into hearing every three minutes I should think. The clack-clack of incendiaries falling, and shrapnel it fell like rain around us.* ('Diary of a Tyseley Housewife', *Mass Observation Archive* cited in Tom Harrisson, *Living Through the Blitz*, London, 1990 edn, p. 203).

The Kent Street premises of Jarrett, Rainsford and Laughton, 21 November 1940.

John Horner was General Secretary of the Fire Brigades Union and he was in Birmingham during the raid. He noticed that there was no main fire zone, rather 'the whole city seemed ablaze'. So many were the fires that some 'were completely unattended'. At others 'single pump crews of AFS men were trying to tackle whole blazing warehouses, while some streets were blocked with pumps wasting precious water on ruins spread over what was nothing but a smouldering devastation'. He believed that there was 'a complete lack of co-ordination and direction', and that the volunteers were hindered because they had not been integrated with regular officers and men'. Others shared his feelings that 'in this night's ordeal most of Birmingham's crews were leaderless', and two days later the Chief Officer of the city's brigade resigned. He was replaced by a fire officer appointed by the Home Office. (John Horner, 'Recollections of a General Secretary', article supplied by Ray Bryant, 29 April 1995).

There were major problems in coping with the havoc wrought by the bombers, but there was also defiance. Ernest Snelgrove was driving his corporation bus when the blitz 'got a little hot'. He asked his passengers to take cover but they persuaded him to carry on to the terminus. He did. After a short break it was a little quieter and Ernest decided that he would complete his run and go back into town to pick up any stragglers. When he saw the flares coming down he 'let her rip with no regard for traffic lights or any other signal'. After taking cover he returned once more to the depot to clock off. It was early in the morning and he walked two miles to reach home. On his arrival 'he found that a high explosive bomb had blown a crater in his back garden, big enough, as he said, to take a tram'. His wife was in the shelter and neighbours had dug her out and brought her to safety. Next door a woman and her son had been killed. Ernest then went down the street to find news about his sister and her daughter-in-law. They were in hospital. ('Devotion to Duty', *Birmingham Mail*, 21 November 1940).

Frank Jones was another brave man. He had just arrived home and was having his tea when the sirens sounded. His wife recalled that:

> He went straight out on duty as a voluntary air raid warden and I took my son to the next-door neighbour's shelter. Bombs were falling all around. At 9 o'clock a warden came for me as my husband was seriously injured. This was on Soho Road, Handsworth where others were killed, including a young man who had survived Dunkirk. Dr Burgess, who then lived on Soho Road, rendered first aid and called for an ambulance. Due to the chaos, it was four hours before an ambulance came to take my husband to hospital. He had multiple injuries. The infection spread, and his right leg was amputated. He spent 15 months in hospital and nine on crutches. Then he was fitted with an artificial limb. He was 36 years-old. The aftermath was blackouts, and strain, which caused coronary heart disease. He died after much suffering at the age of 57. (November 1940. *Evening Mail Special*, November 1980, p.6).

Elsewhere in Handsworth, a bomb fell on 140, Alfred Road. With her mother, two brothers, a sister and a baby nephew, the eight-year old Mary Resuggan was in an Anderson Shelter in the garden. She had no recollection of the explosion, 'I suppose we were temporarily deafened but the shelter door blew in and rubble and shrapnel flew in, narrowly missing my brother's head'. Then 'pandemonium broke loose and we were all screaming for dad and our other brother' who were in the house. The youngster survived. His father's body was found two days later. (November 1940. *Evening Mail Special*, November 1980, p. 6).

Not far away, Patricia Reed and a friend were in the 'Villa Cross' Picture House when the manager told them that they would have to leave because the air raid sirens had begun. They were directed to a shelter across the road, beneath the cellars of some shops. Ignoring the advice and having no sense of danger, the two teenaged girls set off home. They 'ran all the way down Lozells Road, she went left to Finch Road and I carried on to Lozells Street'. They were fortunate. The shelter they had spurned had taken a direct hit, 'and everyone in there had been killed'. (Letter, 1995). Mrs E. Wilson had a similar frightening experience. She was coming out of the 'Orient' Picture House 'when a heavy raid started'. She and her friend sheltered in 'her entry for a while then she decided to go down the shelter to her family'. Mrs Wilson 'ran to my Gran's house in New John Street. I shall never forget that night. Incendiary bombs were dropping, they aimed for Lucas but luckily missed it.' The next morning she went to work and 'passed the entry where we had sheltered but it was no longer there'. Her friend's house had been bombed also, but she survived in the cellar. (Letter, 20 February 1995).

The shattered premises of Frederick's Hairdressers after a naval mine blasted John Bright Street, 21 November 1940. Notice the glass roof of New Street Station in the background.

Frederick Haddon was another person who had a lucky escape. He was walking past the library at Albert Road, Aston when he heard the drone of German planes. A warden told him to go into a 'big shelter'. Because he lived 'only down the road', Frederick told the warden he would be 'okay'. As he reached his entry 'there was a flash and a bang and the shelter had a direct hit'. The warden was blown across the road and into a bush. (Letter, 30 May 1995). It was a terrifying and startling experience to be caught in the open during a raid. When the sirens sounded Miss B. Wright and her brother were in the 'Capitol' Picture House, Ward End, but they could not leave 'because the doors were locked'. An incendiary bomb hit the screen, 'so we got out and ran home' to Alum Rock. As they 'passed the Moat House a bomb hit the Alum Rock Road. Gunfire was belching and barking'. She felt warm fluid running down her chest and shouted. 'Stop, I've been hit!'' Her brother persuaded her to carry on running and when she arrived home she found she was 'soaked in perspiration, not blood'. (Letter, 15 February 1995). Closer to the city centre in Hampton Street, H.J. Blandford was helping to put out the fires which were burning everywhere when a land mine fell in St George's Street. It struck the depot and garage of the Birmingham Mail, demolishing 'an enormous fleet of vans and cars' and causing 'extensive damage to all the houses in the district'. Local families were taken to St George's Church until the all-clear sounded. (*November 1940. Evening Mail Special*, November 1980, p.4).

Over at Camp Hill an unexploded bomb landed by Ravenshurst Street. Like May Golding, women and children in the vicinity were told to leave their shelters and 'were shepherded round to St Anne's Convent in Lowe Street'. The Mother Superior and her nuns 'gave us refreshments and blankets although it was impossible to sleep with the gunfire and explosions', and the next morning they handed 'us all a drink of tea'. When the nearby grocer's shop opened May and her neighbour, Mrs Goodyear, used up their ration coupons and 'bought two quarters of tea, then handed them in the Convent. They blessed us.' (Tom Golding, *96 Years a Brummie, 1889-1986*, Birmingham, 1986, p. 83).

Scenes of destruction abounded in Birmingham. On Holloway Head, the whole of Grant Street was laid waste. Elsie Hall was eighteen and when the air-raid sirens started wailing at 6.55 p.m. she and her widowed mother went to shelter in a reinforced cellar which they shared with neighbours. They heard the planes and the bombs dropping but 'we tried to be cheerful by chatting away, each one trying to forget what was going on outside'. Suddenly a land mine exploded and 'everything went silent for a few moments and we were in complete darkness'. None of them could 'hardly speak as our mouths seemed to be filled with dust'. They clambered out of the cellar grating and 'made our way through the rubble'. The sky was lit up with 'all the action' and mother and daughter 'seemed to be just numbed with fear'. A warden saw them and took them to an Anderson Shelter 'where everyone was so kind and comforting to us'. They remained there until the all clear. When they emerged from their protection they found 'Grant Street flattened'. Like other survivors of the blitz, the only possessions they had were the clothes which they were wearing. (*November 1940. Evening Mail Special*, November 1980, p. 6).

A bus overturned during bombing on Highgate Road, Sparkbrook, 19 November 1940.

Mines also obliterated Berry Road, Alum Rock and Alfred Road in Sparkhill. Not far away Mr A.E. Harrison and a mate were walking close to a house in Highgate Road, Sparkbrook when it was hit by a bomb:

> *With the help of some people who were near we made a good clearing at the cellar grating on the pavement. I managed to get down in the cellar knowing that someone told us there was a family down in the cellar sheltering. As I got down into the shelter, I found it had all caved in. Looking around the brickwork and dust I found the male covered up to his neck in debris. I started to remove it as best I could but after about 10 minutes it became very dangerous on my own. As I got out of the cellar the A.R.P. Rescue Team had arrived. I was asked to hang about after I explained what it was like down in the cellar, but only being 17 at the time I got scared and hopped it quick thinking I should not have gone down in the first place.* (Letter, April, 1995).

Collapsed buildings were a constant danger. So too was flooding. The teenage Denis Howell was a member of the Home Guard and was also deputy group fire guard officer in Wheeler Street, Lozells. On one occasion a high explosive bomb landed in the neighbourhood and caused 'great distress'. It ruptured the main water main and 'a whole family was wiped out' when their cellar was flooded. (Denis Howell, *Made in Birmingham. The Memoirs of Denis Howell*, London, 1990, p. 40). Ann Burke emphasised another hazard. She lived in Washwood Heath and:

> *I also remember a bomb destroyed the Methodist Church Hall in Common Lane. Several families were sheltering in the cellar. They were not killed outright but were trapped beneath the hall where a gas pipe was fractured, and they were slowly gassed before they could be rescued. Two of them were Christine and Jean Baker who were school friends of mine and their father who was caretaker of the church and on firewatch duty that night was talking to them above the ground until they died. It was very sad and I often recall that night.* (Letter, August 1996).

Public Works Department men clearing up after a raid on Birmingham.

Thomas Bradley, a warden, gained the British Empire Medal for saving a man and woman who were trapped in a cellar where 'there was a strong escape of coal-gas'. ('Further Awards for Gallantry', *Birmingham Weekly Post*, 27 June 1941).

The members of rescue parties worked in harrowing circumstances. A secret report to the Office of Home Security detailed some of the disturbing and agonising situations they had to cope with. At about 9.46 p.m. on 19 November a high explosive bomb demolished four houses in James Street, Lozells. A number of people were trapped and as the rescue workers strove to free them another high explosive bomb fell, as did a parachute mine. Every house in James Street was damaged. Wardens and police officers saved several people before two rescue parties and a first aid party arrived from Sidcup Road, Kingstanding. They were led by Foreman Pond and saved four Brummies. The difficult work had to stop at 2.15 a.m. because there was not enough light. Early the next morning two dead children were found in part of an Anderson Shelter which had been blasted to the junction of Johnson Street and Leonard Street. A short time later a torso was uncovered at the rear of 69, Carlyle Road.

At 10.15 a.m. on 20 November a rescue party from Sidcup Road came back to the horrific scene and the bodies of three children were uncovered as were a femur and a hand. All were taken by ambulance to Scott's Mortuary. In the afternoon two dead women were found along with parts of the bodies of a woman and child. They were in a section of an Anderson Shelter which had been blown from 'the direction of James Street' and into the front bedroom of 75, Carlyle Road. Another eight people had been in that shelter. All of them were blown to pieces. The rescue work resumed on the morning of 21 November and three more bodies were recovered. It continued for the next ten days and the foot of a child and that of a woman were found. Seven people from the neighbourhood were still unaccounted for but on 1 December 'it was felt that no useful purpose could be served by the continuance of the search'. Almost a year later, on 14 November 1941, workers were demolishing bomb-damaged houses in Carlyle Road. They uncovered 'human bones lodged in the rafters'. (Celia Hall, 'Search for the human debris of a disaster', *November 1940. Evening Mail Special*, November 1980, p. 16). In such agonising circumstances, one of the most heart-rending jobs was that done by funeral directors. After a single raid, one of them had delivered to him 46 sacks filled with remains, having 'to clean and straighten them up as well as he could and lay them out for identification'. (Harrisson, *Living Through the Blitz*, p. 250).

Pauline Franklin worked as a telegraphist at the General Post Office in Victoria Square. On 19 November she was on the late shift and with her colleagues sheltered in 'The Refuge' in the basement. At 1.10 a.m. the next morning 'there was an almighty thud above us and everyone instinctively threw themselves on the floor'. The lights went out

A Brummie family made homeless by bombing, 16 August 1940.

and 'for what seemed an eternity we could hear heavy items falling above us, followed by complete silence'. Everyone began to talk at once, and 'one girl had hysterics as her father was on the roof fire-watching'. Within minutes 'the people in the first-aid post along the corridor had provided us with cups of tea'. Then the fire-watchers appeared 'covered in dust and hardly recognisable but safe and sound'. The night 'seemed interminable' but about 8.00 a.m. the workers left the building, emerging into New Street:

> and I shall never forget the sight that met my eyes. It was completely covered in hose-pipes and water was flowing everywhere. There was not a pane of glass left in the shop windows. People were still trying to get to work, however, clambering over the hose-pipes and glass. When I arrived at Albert Street I found out the trams could not run because the lines had been bombed along the route. I had to walk all the way home to Stechford and the scene was like one of those films we see of refugees escaping with their few pathetic worldly goods tied in bundles or laden in prams. The people I saw had been bombed out and were trying to get to relatives or to the special offices in town which helped such people find shelter. (Letter, 20 February 1995).

German raiders targeted Birmingham again on 20 November. It was reported that 'the greater part of a street in a working-class district was wrecked by a big bomb'. This was Queens Road, Aston. One woman was killed. The death toll would have been greater had not everyone else packed into the road's cellars. Hilda Greenway, then Pickman, was one of the survivors. With her family she had sheltered in the basement of Atkinson's Brewery and 'as usual, we had a right pasting off Gerry'. When the all clear sounded they went into the street 'and my Mom was mooching in her bag for the front door key, and my sister said, "If you're looking for your key, Mom, I wouldn't bother as there's no glass in the windows, and the front door is over the road in the gutter, but don't worry we won't be cold as Gerry has dropped an oil bomb in the coal yard and it's lovely and warm in our house".' (Letter, 27 June 1996).

The explosive which mangled Queen's Road was a naval mine. Another smashed up John Bright Street. Such devices were between six and nine feet in length and weighed about 1,000lbs. Carried by parachutes, they exploded close to the ground to maximise the damage they caused. If they did not detonate immediately they were approached by Royal Navy mine disposal officers such as Lieutenant Horace Taylor and Sub-Lieutenant Russon. On to the fuse of a mine they attached a specially adapted motor horn, pumping it up 'to create the same pressure as 12 feet of sea water'. This made the explosive safe for a time and allowed the officers to 'work on the magnetic or acoustic fuses'. On the morning of the 20 November the two officers defused such a mine outside Baskerville House and then went on to another at Reginald Road, Saltley. As they were working, its clock began to tick. Abandoning his operations Lieutenant Taylor had just reached the front door when he was blasted three streets away. After he recovered from his wounds he returned to active service and was awarded the George Cross. (Clem Lewis, 'When death floated down on a patch of silk', November 1940. Evening Mail Special, November 1980, p. 13).

Not every unexploded bomb expert survived. May Golding's husband was an ex-soldier and had witnessed death and destruction on a massive scale in the Great

War. A postman based at Walford Road, Sparkhill, he told his wife that:

> *following an overnight raid during which the sound of bombs not far away were heard, he started to walk to work about half past four. As he neared Walford Road death and chaos met him. A high explosive bomb had fallen near the corner of Walford Road and Stratford Road. I believe a disposal squad expert in trying to defuse the bomb had been killed with his remains strewn about. Werffs, the fashion dress shop on the corner of Walford Road was badly damaged. The scattered dresses and broken models were a sorry mess. My husband took a torn dress or two from the open shop, retrieving a shattered leg from the road, then wrapped the limb in the remnants of the dresses. The bundle was placed in the care of a policeman to be dealt with by the ambulance men.* (Golding, *96 Years a Brummie*, pp. 84-5).

This incident was remembered clearly by Our Dad.

There was a respite on the night of 21 November, but the next evening a force of 200 bombers attacked Birmingham. In his diary Ernest Price wrote that it was a 'Clear Sky. Devastating Raid on City. Land-Mines, Bombs & Incendiaries on all districts. Places Damaged - B.S.A., Singer, Wright's Ropes, Lawley St Goods. General & Selly Oak Hosp. Was on Duty.' The Germans themselves declared that 'owing to the favourable weather all kinds of attacks could be carried out. Single raiders and mass formations followed each other and for the first time 'a large number of low level attacks were carried out on Birmingham'. The communiqué stated that the raid was 'concentrated on those armament works which up to now had not been hit by German bombs', but admitted that as well as factories 'whole streets . . . are destroyed and gutted by fire'. ('German Version', *Birmingham Mail*, 23 November 1940).

The wreckage inside the burnt-out Hockley Bus Garage, 22 November, 1940.

The raid began just before 7.00 p.m. and lasted almost eleven hours. At 11.00 p.m. it was reported that 'the raids continue with great intensity. Fire situation serious. Some factories of importance hit. Large blocks of houses demolished, 38 in. gas main in Lancaster Street still alight.' The city's ordeal was not over. At midnight more bombers spat out death and desolation. They were followed by another wave of attackers at 3.00 a.m.. They swept to and fro over the city from Acocks Green in the south east to Handsworth in the north west. At Snow Hill Station there were many Welsh people waiting to go home to the Valleys for the weekend. George Buffery was there with them and as the bombs began to fall 'panic set in, in the underground part of the station'. Then 'all at once the Welsh mass choir sang out'. It was 'a beautiful sound, so calming'. (Celia Hall, 'Night of Horror', *November 1940. Evening Mail Special,* November 1980, p. 3; Margaret Buffery, Letter, 15 February 1995).

Over 600 fires were started, many of them big, and every available man and pump was in action. The Gas Offices in Edmund Street were destroyed and Hockley Bus Garage went up. On some roads so great was the heat that the tarmac was alight. The situation deteriorated rapidly when three trunk water mains on the Bristol Road were fractured by high explosive bombs and 'all at once nearly the whole city was without water'. Fire fighters desperately looked for water in canals and bomb craters but the position was critical. (Klopper, *The Fight Against Fire,* p.90). Peter Woodbridge and his widower dad lived with his grandmother Sara Woodbridge in a back-to-back in Baker Street, Small Heath - in the line of attack. His gran would not go into any shelter during the raid.

On the Friday night in question, she sat on top of the cellar steps in the pantry, with myself as a young lad together with my younger sister, each of us were under my

grandmother's arms, while all the pots and pans were falling off the pantry shelves on top of us. On that night alone there were seven people killed in Baker Street who were in a shelter cellar just a few doors away . . . The next morning we all had to go and collect water bringing it back in buckets from the main railway sidings in Bolton Road. This was because the main water supply to Birmingham had been hit by a bomb during the night. (Letter, April 1995).

In Tyseley a B.S.A. dispersal factory was bombed, as was the main B.S.A. works in Armoury Road where everyone was ordered to leave the premises. Mrs E. George was an evacuee who had just returned to her home in Colebrook Road, Greet. Taking shelter in Albion Road

Fighting fires in New Street, 25 October 1940. At the end of the street, notice the Times Building; it is now Waterstone's. The hoses are aimed at buildings which were to be destroyed on 9 April 1941.

'everyone there tried to cheer each other up, singing and playing cards.' Then the police arrived to tell them that the B.S.A. had been hit. They had to move to another shelter and as they came outside 'the flames lit up the whole area'. Suddenly they heard planes overhead and 'Mom and Dad covered me and there was an explosion nearby as a bomb hit close to Greet School'. (Local History Study Group, Golden Hillock School, *Birmingham Citizens: The Experience of War. Study I. Growing Up in Wartime Birmingham*, Birmingham, 1995).

After the raid the local newspapers announced neither the fracturing of the water mains nor a report which stated that the city's Water Department needed at least five days to make good the damage to them. The situation was critical and Brum's authorities sent a message to the Ministry of Home Security in London. It explained that only one-fifth of Birmingham's water supply was available and that a regional call had been made for all possible water cars to be placed at the disposal of Birmingham Water Department. Other arrangements were made. A company of Royal Engineers was called in and made ready to explode fire breaks if they were necessary. Sixty pumps were sent to Birmingham from London and elsewhere and 250 men were drafted into the city. Other major appliances were placed by small water supplies on the edge of Brum. Klopper has called these emergency measures 'pitifully inadequate', adding that senior fire officers 'knew that another heavy raid on the city would be catastrophic'. On the night of 23 November Brum was almost defenceless and 'had the enemy struck again immediately there is little doubt that Birmingham would have been practically destroyed by fire'. (Klopper, *The Fight Against Fire*, p.90). Edwin Webb and John Duncan have reinforced the danger faced by Brummies. The lack of water meant that major blazes could have spread 'producing the ideal conditions for a firestorm - such as that which completely destroyed Dresden later in the war'. (Webb and Duncan, *Blitz Over Britain*, p. 79). Thankfully the *Luftwaffe* did not resume its crippling attacks until 3 December. During that time the trunk mains were repaired, the city's fire brigade was reorganised, and co-ordination was established between the regulars and the A.F.S.

Although Brummies were not informed officially of the direness of the situation, they realised it themselves. Doreen Harris M.B.E. worked at the Wesleyan and General Assurance Company:

> *Once we were bombed all night. No trams could run from Erdington to town. We walked all the way . . . the centre of Birmingham was covered with broken glass, the gas pipes had all been damaged, water everywhere. We were told that if they came that night we would be finished. We went*

Women in Aston salvaging a kettle and other belongings from their wrecked home, 19 November 1940.

into the office to be told a delayed action bomb was sitting there. (Letter, 11 August 1996).

Evelyn Smith had a similar memory. She was employed at Walter Austin's, 'a high class ladies shop', and she had to walk to town from Acocks Green. When she arrived there 'was such excitement and concern - an unexploded land mine was buried on Lewis's corner adjoining Bull Street'. She and her colleagues were directed to St Philip's churchyard where they joined workers from Bells and Scotches and other retailers. As she was a junior, Evelyn was sent to Pattison's Restaurant and Cake Shop 'to buy farthing buns - buy a dozen and you had one free'. They munched their way through dozens, until the bomb was made safe: 'how naive we were, chatting and laughing the hours away, not fully comprehending that if the bomb had exploded sitting in the churchyard would not have been the safest place'. (Letter, 22 February 1995).

At least 682 Brummies were killed during the raids of 19-22 November. Another 1,087 were injured seriously and many more were slightly hurt. These were not the only casualties. No-one has ever found out how many spirits were scarred for ever,

MEALS SERVICE.—A centre at which hot meals may be bought cheaply for consumption off the premises was opened on Wednesday at Summer Lane Council School.

how many dreams were broken, and how many lives were ruined. The human cost was matched by the destruction of property. Nearly 2,000 houses were smashed to pieces and thousands more were damaged seriously. Dot Harris, then Nock, and her brother were toddlers in Gooch Street, Highgate when 'we were bombed out and Mom saved us both by throwing herself on top of us on the settee'. Her mother, Mable, 'tried to put bits together for us to start again after the war, but once again the public house belonging to friends where she stored them was a direct hit and friends and belongings were lost'. (Letter, 1995). Hazel Denham, then Andrews, experienced the same kind of loss. Her family's home in White Street, Balsall Heath 'was bombed down - after mom, my two sisters & myself were dug out, we were taken to Evesham Hospital'. When they returned to Brum they stayed first 'with mom's one sister & then her other sister'. Finally they moved into a house in Dolobran Road, Sparkbrook. (Letter, 27 February 1995).

Phyllis Arnold was prepared for the possibility of homelessness when her house in Erdington was ruined. Each night when the sirens wailed she took with her into the shelter 'a blue bird toffee box containing birth certificates and numerous policies'. In her opinion one of the other worst aspects of the war was 'the daily thought of what I had to give my children to eat'. She recalled that 'every time a ship was sunk bringing in food, we all worried', and she brought to mind 'the whale meat, 2s 6d a lb, which looked like liver and was best cooked with onions'. Often she queued for just one tomato 'and sliced it up thinly so that 5 of us could have a slice'. (Letter, May 1995). Gordon Bowen had a war-time meal he has 'never forgotten'. One day at Turfpits Junior School, Erdington 'we were told that we were in for a treat, and what a treat it turned out to be'. Australian schoolchildren had sent cans of food. Gordon was given three cans, one of which was stewed steak. His sister 'knocked up some pastry' and made a pie with the meat, which they ate with 'some spuds and cabbage'. (Letter, September 1996).

In the districts most ruined by bombing, many people had no facilities to cook food. Because of this the city's Emergency Committee asked the Education Department to open centres where hot meals could be bought cheaply for eating off the premises. The first to do so was at Summer Lane Schools, on 13 December 1940. Two-course meals costing 8d were served between 12 noon and 2.00 p.m. They consisted of meat and vegetables and a pudding, although soup and other food was available at lower prices. One of the meals was Exeter Stew. In total 40lbs of potatoes, 20lbs of beef, 15lbs of carrots 'and proportionate weights of other things' were used to make enough for each day. ('Communal Meals, *Birmingham Post*, 31 December 1940).

Sanded Legs and Shrapnel: Life Carries on in the Blitz

Even in the worst raids, people showed determination, obstinacy and resilience. And despite the deaths they still struggled to celebrate life. On Saturday 23 November Bert Hook was to be married at St Paul's Church, Lozells. Because of the danger in her neighbourhood, his fiancée had left her home and was staying with relatives in

Great Barr. Consequently, 'on her wedding morning she walked from there through debris & rubbish to William Street, Lozells, as public transport had stopped'. When she arrived she was told she could not go into her house as a time bomb had dropped in Gerard Street. Explaining that it was her wedding day, the wardens allowed her 30 minutes 'to get in and out again'. Arriving at the church they found it had been bombed and they were sent to St Mathias's Church, Hockley. By mistake Bert's mom and dad went to St Matthew's,

Marriage of Ivy Bagley and Walter Jackson, 27 January 1940 at Christchurch, Yardley Wood. There was four foot of snow on the ground and after the wedding Walter embarked for France. He returned from Dunkirk and was then posted to Egypt and India. Ivy did not see him for six years and seven months.

Handsworth 'causing a long delay in the ceremony'. The photographer was not informed of the change of church and 'but for a relative's Brownie Box camera we would have missed our only photograph'. Kunzles catered for the reception at Gower Street School and it 'went off well, despite the fact that as the water mains had been hit, nobody could have a cup of tea - and other drinks were in short supply too!' For their honeymoon the couple were allowed 'one day's holiday which we spent browsing round Woolworth's buying bits & pieces for our new home'. (Letter, 16 July 1996).

Frank Lloyd actually clicked with his wife Annie during an air raid. On 12 November 1940 both of them were at the 'Winson Green' Picture House, Winson Green Road.

> *How we met? She sat behind me in the picture house and I was in uniform (army) age 17 yrs. She was 16 yrs. She kept on putting her foot on my seat at the back of me, so I took off her shoe. I did give it back to Annie. 10.15 p.m. an air raid was announced on the screen. She and her friend left, I followed them home to Marroway St. She looked at me & then I asked for a date. She was a trainee telephone eng. 1940 when I was on leave we went to her home after going to the pictures and we found Marroway St (Northbrook St end) blocked off and about 4 ARP Wardens on duty. Her parents, 2 sisters, and brother had been taken down to St Cuthbert's Church, Winson Green Rd. The warden said an unexploded bomb was behind her parent's house. The bomb went off next morning at 7.15 a.m. Their house was littered onto the pavement. They went into lodgings for a few months then they were offered a house at Paget Rd Pype Hayes. We married 24 July 1943 at the B'ham Registrar . . . We have always loved each other.* (Letter, 1995).

As A. Morton explained in the midst of 'tear, sweat and toil' there were 'some good times also, such as making your own enjoyment, going dancing to the tune of the Lambeth Walk, Roll-out-the-barrel'. (Letter, 17 February 1995). The favourite dances of Len Yates were more modern. He preferred 'the Jive & Be Bop & Jitterbugging', and went dancing at the West End with Sonny Rose's Band, or at the Casino with Teddy Foster's Band. (Letter, 27 February 1995). There were other major dance halls and hundreds of smaller venues. Vic Jones was one of the musicians who played at a variety of them. Aged fifteen at the outbreak of war, he was apprenticed at a factory which made briar pipes. Three times a week he visited 25 tobacconist's 'to collect and deliver pipe repairs'. He saw most of 'the previous night's damage in the city centre' yet 'it was amazing how we carried on just as normal'. When he was not on fire watch, 'I towed my drums in a trailer behind my bicycle, to play for dancing'. He was never in a regular band, but joined with other part-time musicians where he was wanted. Sometimes an air raid would begin but 'if the dancers wanted to carry on (and a big majority of them were in uniform and did not want to waste their leave) we kept on playing for them until 11.00 p.m. with our fingers crossed'. Sometimes it took 'over an hour to cycle home' to Hingeston Street, Brookfields via 'craters, fires, hosepipes across the roads, diversions for unexploded H.E.s etc'. (Letter, 1995).

Unable to buy nylons in Britain, young women did whatever they could to make their legs appear stockinged for their nights out. Some rubbed on wet sand, but Iris Gibson 'personally painted my legs with still obtainable gravy browning liquid - the mind boggles at the mere thought now, and great dexterity was needed to get that black seam straight with the aid of an eyebrow pencil'. (Letter, 11 February 1995). Later in the war a woman could get hold of nylons only if she had an American soldier as a boyfriend. Unsurprisingly the better paid G.I.s were popular. Hilda Burnett and her friend were sauntering along Bristol Street one Sunday afternoon and 'walking towards us were two Yanks'. She said to her mate, 'Watch me', and as they passed she called out the familiar words, 'Hi Joe, what do you know?' One of the Americans turned and came back, stating 'I don't know much babe, but what I do know is worth talking about'. The two young women 'fell about in fits of laughter, needless to say we did not meet them coming back'. (Letter, 3 May 1995).

Doris Evans stressed that 'with all the shortages during the war it was very hard trying to look glamorous and we had to resort to all sorts of tricks to achieve it'. Her mom had a second-hand clothes shop and one of the articles she bought was a leopard skin coat. Of the three daughters,

Workers trying to clear up the rubble of Queens Road, Aston, the morning of 21 November 1940.

Vi offered the most - making Dot and Rene 'very jealous'. But the coat was riddled with moth holes and began to crumble. Vi was 'clever with her hands' and as nothing was thrown away in the war, out of the good parts of a moth-eaten leopard skin coat 'she made herself a very fetching pill box hat and handbag to match'. Her husband was in the army and she stayed in most evenings, but one night she had a rare treat with her workmates. She looked 'so glamorous in a black coat and this hat perched at a very fetching angle over one eye, with this nifty handbag and her hair in a long page-boy style'. Her pal Rose was green with envy and the following night she begged to borrow the hat and bag for her date with an American. The next morning Rose was late for work, arriving with eyes red-rimmed and a thick lip.

> Vi said, 'whatever happened to you, Rose, did you bump into the lamp-post?' (A very easy thing to do in the black out). Rose with tears rolling down her face gave Vi the bag and said, 'Before you look in it please let me explain what happened last night.' Apparently this wonderful Yank had taken her for a drink or two - possibly three, then they went to have a fish and chip supper at a nice restaurant in town. As he was walking her home he got very amorous and tried to get his wicked way with her. She said she had a terrible struggle with him and when he realised he wasn't going to get what he wanted from her, he smacked her in the mouth (hence the fat lip) and then Rose said between sobs that he snatched off her head the lovely

leopardskin hat and tore it into shreds, threw it on the ground and wiped his feet on it. Well Vi said nothing but we never did have another Leopardskin coat come into the shop. (Letter, 1995).

Entertainment was limited but it was inventive and often took place on afternoons. Miss G.L. Bryant saw the Sadler's Wells Ballet perform 'Giselle' at the 'Theatre Royal' and attended an orchestral concert conducted by Leslie Howard; whilst Margaret W. Farrand went to 'Plays in the Park, 'an open air entertainment, but the weather beat it that often so they were performed under canvas'. She saw 'The Farmer's Wife' and 'Arms and the Man' and at 'The Prince of Wales' Theatre she watched 'The Chocolate Soldier'. Each Sunday afternoon she listened to the City of Birmingham Symphony Orchestra performing under George Weldon at the Town Hall, and she attended a 'Worker's Playtime' at the 'West End' Dance Hall. (Letters, 23 February 1995 and 20 February 1995). This was a lunch-time concert which went out live on the radio from a different place each week day. Another was put on at the canteen of the B.S.A. in Armoury Road. Peter Hemming was an apprentice electrician at the factory and was in charge of the stage lighting and sound system. The two main turns were Jimmy Jewel and Ben Warris on this 'very popular programme' which was 'a morale booster'. (Letter, 25 July 1996).

Boys playing in a crater near a public shelter in Aston, just missed by a bomb, 17 May 1941.

For youngsters, the war was horrific but also it was adventurous. Jim Oliver lived in Coleshill Street, not far from the Law Courts in Corporation Street. He and his mates 'often walked around town looking at the bombed buildings - we even played on them'. On one occasion they were larking about in a damaged house in Park Street 'and we were running along a pathway between the rubble when we came upon a large bomb'. They grabbed stones and threw them at the explosive, fortunately missing their target. Until it filled with rubbish, the local kids also swam in 'a very large tank' in which water was stored in case of fire. (Letter, July 1996). Olive Brown was another child who found the war exciting even though it was a time of horror and sadness. She lived in Camden Street, Brookfields and witnessed Bulpitt's go up 'into the biggest blaze I have ever seen', but like the other kids she 'used to search for bits of shrapnel among the rubble after the bombing'. (Letter, 15 March 1996).

Then six years old, Dave Martin lived in Solihull Road, Sparkhill. Nearby on the Stratford Road there was a cycle shop which had been bombed out. He, his older brother Tony and some mates scrambled into the ruins, hunting for shrapnel on the site. They found a live incendiary - knowing it was unexploded because it was whole, whereas when such a device exploded all that was left was the base. They took it to 'some lad's shed, placed it in the vice and hit it with hammers to set it off'. Luckily it did not explode and the boys placed the incendiary in a bucket and took it to Sparkhill police station. When they appeared in the door the sergeant disappeared out the back. The lads then took the bucket to the fire station in Court Road, where it was defused. Mr Martin 'didn't half belt us when we got home'. (Interview, 22 August 1996).

Dances, pubs, the pictures, the theatre, war-time football all drew in crowds, but many people stayed at home for their entertainment. Like Mr J.M. Gardiner they charged up the accumulator and listened to the wireless: 'what laughs we had and that was what kept our spirits up during those dark days - the radio!' His favourite show was ITMA, 'It's That Man Again', with Tommy Handley; 'then there was Variety Bandbox with alternately Derek Roy and the great Frankie Howard'. (Letter, 1995). Each morning at 7.00 the news was read and on Tuesdays it was followed by 'Bing Sings'. John Spittle recalled that the 'young bloods cursed Hitler for arranging a surfeit of news for Tuesday morning thus limiting the number of Bing records that could be played'. (Letter, 11 January 1996).

Churchill's speeches were one of the major attractions of the radio. As on 4 June 1940 his words inspired the nation through the bleak days which followed Dunkirk.

> We shall not flag or fail. We shall go on to the end. We shall fight on the seas and the oceans, we shall fight with growing confidence and growing strength in the air. We shall defend our island whatever the cost may be. We shall fight on the beaches, we shall fight on the landing grounds, we shall fight in the fields and in the streets, we shall fight in the hills; we shall never surrender. ('Mr Churchill's Speeches', Birmingham Weekly Post, 29 November 1940).

There was a less stirring but equally effective way in which morale was kept high, especially amongst men. This was through 'the exploits of "Jane", the Queen of the Cartoon Strips'. She appeared each morning in the Daily Mirror and was the creation of Norman Pett, a tutor at Moseley Road School of Art and Design in Balsall Heath, Birmingham. The model for the character was Christobel Leighton-Porter because 'Pett's wife was a golf fanatic and wasn't always available'. Pett taught Gordon Holden, whose prized possession 'is a 1944 copy of 'Pett's Annual' devoted to a lady who teased, tantalised and lost her dress at the least provocation. Jane went to war painted on tanks, bren-gun carriers, military vehicles, warship and flew with the RAF Bomber Crews over enemy territory, even though the Air Council frowned on "Nose Art".' (Letter, 8 April 1995).

Not Downhearted: the Winter of 1940

By late November 1940 the shopping and civic centre of Birmingham was scarred deeply by the bombing. So too were most of the central working-class neighbourhoods. Yet even in supposedly safe areas there had been destruction and deaths. Irene Davis remembered a bomb falling on Yardley Wood Station. As they heard the whine before the thud of it landing, she and her mother 'tried to dive under the sofa which only had a 4 inch gap. Now I was 10st and Mom was 12st so no way could we manage that and we ended up on one heap on the floor crying with laughter.' (Letter, 21 February 1995). In Harborne an approved school had been damaged by incendiary bombs, as had the Home of the Little Sisters of the Poor. ('Scars of War', *Birmingham Mail*, 9 December 1940). Later in the war both the Dog's Home in High Street and St John's Church were hit. Win Holt recalled these blasts 'as a terrible time, the screaming of the bombs coming right down over our heads, then the sounds of the fire engines, bells ringing as they raced to the scene, smoke and flames billowing up into the sky'. (Win Holt, *Up The Hill To Harborne*, Birmingham, no date, p. 12).

Bomb damage in Acocks Green, 24 August 1940. Twenty-three people were in the back rooms of these two houses. Fortunately none were injured.

Not far away in Selly Oak, explosives destroyed much of Katie Road; a woodyard in Cotteridge went up in flames; and in Stirchley, the Bournville Lane canal bridge took a direct hit.

Two nursing sisters were killed at the Woodlands Hospital in Northfield, when three bombs hit the building as they were eating their supper; and the Fever Hospital at Little Bromwich was also hit - although no-one was hurt. ('How Birmingham Was Battered in the Blitz', *Birmingham Post Supplement*, 8 May 1945). Further to the west, a high explosive dropped in the residential district of Rotton Park. Two houses were damaged badly and in one of them a married couple were trapped. Police Constable Frederick Miles joined Wardens Robert Strangward and John Gandy, both of Twyning Road. They climbed into the house and heard groaning 'from underneath a large heap of masonry and debris, three to four feet deep'. Digging and delving they brought out a woman from her bed and returned to save her husband. As the men worked, 'there was grave possibility that the house might collapse' and bury them. The three rescuers were awarded the British Empire Medal. ('Birmingham Men Honoured', *Birmingham Post*, 20 September 1941).

The widespread effects of the German air raids are emphasised by the records of

Warden Post E.24A in Yardley. This sector included parts of Church Road, Stoney Lane, Queens Road and Barrows Lane, and it took in all of Vibart Road, Farnol Road, Home Croft, Blakemere Avenue, Wroxton Road, Croft Road, Patrick Road, Jara Road, Charminster Avenue, Buckingham Road and Heathmere Avenue. Collated by John V. Abbott, the information on this neighbourhood shows damage to numerous houses. It also indicates harm done nearby, such as when much of Lily Road was obliterated on 14 November 1940 and twelve people died. A week later two explosives and an oil bomb dropped on Rockingham Road and Charminster Avenue, killing three people. One of them 'was an unfortunate young woman who had been bombed out of her own home only a few days previously, and had sought refuge with friends'. (John V. Abbott, *Raiders Past. Air Raids on Yardley*, Studley, 1993, p. 25).

Bombers did not respect neat distinctions made by the authorities between vulnerable and less vulnerable districts. Nor should it be forgotten that numerous men and women from relatively unscathed districts were workers or A.R.P. volunteers in those areas battered by the *Luftwaffe*. One of them was Frank Popplewell of Marston Green. As a railway clerk he was on the early shift at Hockley Goods Station, and in the afternoons he became a porter. Each weekend he was out with the St John's Ambulance Brigade, and once a month he fire-watched at G.W.R. warehouses in Winson Green, Soho and Hockley. There were many others like Frank, people who came from the outskirts of Brum to help their fellows in the central neighbourhoods. They included the people who saved Mrs M. Hughes. In November 1940 she and

her husband were trapped in their shelter in Highfield Road, Sparkhill. They were dug out by members of a rescue party from Hall Green. (April 1940. *Evening Mail Special*, April 1980, pp. 5-7).

Demolition of houses following a raid in Knowle Road, Sparkhill, close to the Stratford Road, 18 October 1940. In the background is the Springfield Social Club in Solihull Road.

Large numbers of suburban A.R.P. workers died in carrying out their duties. From mid-October to the end of December 1940, fifteen A.F.S. men were honoured in their official journal. Five of them came from places which endured heavy raids - Balsall Heath, Nechells, Small Heath and Washwood Heath. Two were from localities where there was some bombing - Winson Green and Selly Oak. And the other eight were from spots which were mostly unaffected by explosions and fires - Perry Barr, Kingstanding, Stockland Green, Castle Bromwich, Moseley, Yardley Wood and Kings

Heath. ('Roll of Honour, *Squirt. The Official Journal of the Birmingham and Dudley Auxiliary Fire Service*, November 1940, p. 5 and February 1941, p. 22, thanks to John Shepherd). **Brummies were united against the Nazi aggressor, whatever their background and wherever they lived. They gave of themselves to help those in need.** Denis Howell 'cannot recall that anyone believed there was anything heroic in this service and this sacrifice. It was a community of free people asserting its rights to existence, with no thoughts of defeat, nor doubts about duty. One million citizens united to defend their freedom.' (Howell, *Made in Birmingham*, p.41).

Anguish and pain were spread across Birmingham and so were daring and selflessness. Still it was the central, working-class districts which were hammered the most by the bombers. They suffered more agonies as Christmas approached. The *Luftwaffe's* raids resumed on the evening of 3 December when 50 bombers pounded the city. Thirty-six people were killed and 60 were injured severely. Major fires erupted in Ashted Row, Moor Street and Bradford Street, where the premises of Fisher and Ludlow's were hit. As the raiders left Birmingham they blasted the Kings Norton Factory Centre, but the fires there 'did not prove to be serious'. Once again the water supply gave concern, and although the main trunks and feeders were unaffected many of the secondary mains were still unrepaired from previous raids. (Jubilee 1935-1985. *50 Year History of Birmingham/West Midlands Fire Service Headquarters*, Birmingham, 1985, p. 37).

Wreckage was widespread and on one battered house were chalked the defiant words 'Blown Out But Not Thrown Out'. ('Birmingham Raid', *Birmingham Mail*, 4 December 1940). The next night the raiders returned. Explosives hit St Andrew's, the ground of Birmingham City Football Club, and wrecked one of the stands; and they destroyed a

Fire-fighters at St Andrew's, the ground of Birmingham City Football Club, in Small Heath, 5 December 1940.

pub in which 20 people had been sheltering. The emergency services saved all of them, apart from the licensee who had been leading his customers in community singing as the bomb fell. The morning after the destruction 'his young son was to be seen wandering pathetically among the ruins and holding beneath his coat his dog, which had been rescued from what remained of the structure'. ('Saved from Debris', *Birmingham Mail*, 5 December 1940).

A week later Brummies endured the longest raid of the war. Two hundred bombers blasted the city for over thirteen hours. They killed 263 people and injured gravely 245 others. Lilian Brooks, then Dugmore, remembered the sirens going about 6.00 p.m. on 11 December. This was followed by the all clear, another warning and 'this went on all night, in and out of the Anderson Shelter'. Exhausted, her mom and dad said, 'no more, we are staying in the house'.

> *Mother started to get the youngest ready for bed, when an almighty bang happened. It went dark and a force of great power lifted me up and through the large window & placed me on my feet . . . A landmine had landed 3 gardens away. 14 people were killed that night. A young girl about 18 was wandering about in our garden asking me in a daze if I had seen her brother. He was 5, afterwards he was found to be one of the victims. She had left the shelter to take him to the outside toilet. The blast just took him away. Her mother was on ARP duty. Her dad, still in the kitchen, was killed. Her name was Christine . . . People came from nowhere, police and first-aid helpers. My family were all safe. We went down the garden to the shelter and found the back had fallen on to the bunks and cut them in half - had we been in there at least 3 of us would have died.* (Letter, 1995).

The Congregational Church in Stoney Lane, Sparkhill was wrecked. When it was hit by a landmine 159 people were in a shelter across the road. Fortunately none were injured. Amongst the other churches damaged were St Mary's, Acocks Green, St Peter's, Harborne and St Anne's, Moseley. ('How Birmingham Was Battered in the Blitz', *Birmingham Post Supplement*, 8 May 1945). St Thomas's, Bath Row took a direct hit. Huge pieces of masonry were thrown over the churchyard, and old oak beams 'which had stood for more than 100 years, snapped like matchsticks'. Tombstones were torn up and 'flung about as if they were so many pebbles'. The pipes of the organ were twisted into grotesque shapes, whilst the keyboard was unrecognisable. All that was left of the church was the bell tower over the main entrance in Granville Street. ('Birmingham Area Raided', *Birmingham Mail*, 13 December 1940).

The next day, on 12 December, King George VI made an 'unheralded' visit to Brum, 'but somehow the news of his presence in the city had spread from place to place included in the itinerary'. According to a reporter from the *Birmingham Post*, 'in mean streets in congested areas, people who have lost their homes and their all swarmed around their King, encouraged by his presence and sympathy. They cheered him to the echo, and spontaneously sang the National Anthem as he hurried on to the next place of call.' This was a major factory 'engaged in war work'. From there he was driven 'to streets in the Aston district that show severe signs of enemy ruthlessness'. The local folk crowded around the king, with children touching him for luck. Here and elsewhere he chatted to survivors. Mrs Warner and John Stanton both told him that Anderson Shelters had saved their lives; 86 year old Mrs Lawson recounted how she had received a facial wound; and a Mrs Ashford informed him she had been dug out of her home when it was blow up, adding 'But we are not downhearted'. After congratulating seventeen-year old David Sharpalls on his bravery in saving lives, the King returned to the city centre. Here he met Ram Singh Bhatra, a Sikh who was in the A.F.S. ('The King Sees Ruined Homes', *Birmingham Post*, 13 December 1940).

King George VI and Lord Mayor Alderman Martineau talking to Brummies, probably in Queens Road, Aston, 12 December 1940.

In his thoughtful book on the Blitz, Tom Harrisson has written that the Blitz on Birmingham began after that on Coventry on 14 November 1940. It did not. Birmingham had endured the Blitz from 9 August. Despite this inaccuracy, Harrisson makes clear the resilience of Brummies in the late autumn and winter of 1940. He admired their strength and perseverance, stressing that 'through thick and thin, most people kept as much as they could of their ordinary cool in extraordinary times'. He also quotes a report by the Research and Experiments Department in the Ministry of Home Security. Written in 1942 it assessed the situation in Brum after the November and December attacks. It considered that more heavy raids could have led to 'a dissolution of the civic entity' and rendered Birmingham almost uninhabitable. (Harrisson, *Living Through the Blitz*, pp. 247-9).

Certainly the dire shortage of water meant that the city could have become a fire-ravaged wasteland. More controversially, the researchers claimed that Birmingham was caught unawares in November whilst the December raids disclosed 'grave deficiencies' in the local A.R.P. system. Few people would disagree that there were problems. Early in November 1940, Alderman Theodore Pritchett had declared that 'the people of Birmingham have not received the protection they should have when the bombers get here'. In particular, he was dissatisfied that the civic authorities had not done all that was possible 'to organise the defence of the city'. Deficiencies in A.R.P. organisation were highlighted later that month when hundreds of homeless people were without food for 24 hours and when there were no instructions available as to how folk could obtain water. (Stanley Warner, 'Our darkest days', *Birmingham Goes to War. 50th Anniversary 1939-1989, Evening Mail Special*, 14 August 1989, p. 15).

It is inconceivable that there would have been no difficulties given the heavy and sustained bombing of the *Luftwaffe* over a short period. Severe strains were placed on the city's A.R.P. and to have expected otherwise is folly. Apart from London and Liverpool, no other British city experienced the same pounding as did Brum. To belittle the bravery and endurance of volunteers and regulars in the emergency services is to fail to recognise the disastrous situation with which they were faced between 19-22 November. Exhausted, hungry and distressed they may have been. Demoralised, dejected and despairing they were not. Night after night they went out and dealt with chaos and carnage. They did not desert their posts, nor did they abandon their duties. They stayed firm and true.

Their resilience was matched by the fortitude of the great majority of Brummies. Like their fellows in other British towns and cities, they withstood with stoicism the anxieties and horrors of the Blitz. Since the Second World War their resolution and tenacity has been disputed by some writers. These researchers have sought to diminish the achievement of ordinary folk in facing up to violence and in maintaining decency. They have emphasised that each night there was

Ruined houses in Birmingham, 28 October 1940.

a flight to the countryside from areas targeted by the *Luftwaffe*. There is no doubt that some people left to stay with friends or family, or that others searched for peace in village pubs or secluded lanes. And who could blame them? For months the citizens of Birmingham, London, Liverpool, Southampton, Portsmouth, Plymouth, Hull and elsewhere had to endure deathly raids and the apprehension of such fearful attacks. It is not surprising that there were those who were desperate for safety and who left their homes. What is more surprising is that most folk remained, knowing that the bombers would return and fully aware that it might be their turn next.

These revisionist writers also assert that the spirit of the Blitz is a myth because there were instances of looting. Reports in the Birmingham Mail indicate that there were men and women who tried to profit from the misery of others. Yet what is striking is that there were so few cases of looting. Everywhere houses were damaged and abandoned. Everywhere there were shops with doors and locks blown to smithereens. Everywhere there were factories with gaping holes. And still few of these places were robbed. There was not a widespread breakdown of law and order. It would be foolish and wrong not to acknowledge the criminal activity of a tiny minority. It is equally foolish and wrong to believe that the great majority of the citizens of the United Kingdom did not behave with dignity, steadfastness and honour during the Blitz. On 18 June 1940, Winston Churchill spoke to the British people following the fall of France. He urged them to brace themselves for their duties and so bear themselves that 'if the British Empire and its Commonwealth lasts for a thousand years, men will still say, "This was their finest hour".' In every blitzed town and city people rose to his words. Bravely, firmly and honestly they stood against evil. It was their finest hour. ('The Ones Who Got Away', *November 1940. Evening Mail Special*, November 1980, p.18; 'To Deter Others', *Birmingham Mail*, 5 December 1940; Charles Eade, compiled, *The War Speeches of the Rt Hon Winston Churchill. Volume I*, London, no date, p. 207).

Sticking It Out: the Raids of 1941-2

The December raids were followed by a long lull. This was interrupted by three raids on 1 January, 4 February and 11 of March 1941, when Ernest Price noted that there were bombs 'over Selly Oak & Handswth. 9 Jerries down'. Peter Donnelly's father was killed in this attack. A survivor of trenches in the First World War, Dennis Francis Donnelly was fire watching in Millhouse Road, South Yardley:

> *He was only 44 years of age. I cannot remember much of my father's Requiem Mass. I do recall my brother served at the altar. My strongest memories, however, are of the funeral itself: seeing my father's coffin covered in the red, white and blue of the Union Jack and an officer of my father's former regiment helping my tear-torn mother into the large black funeral car, and the long, long, tortuous drive to the cemetery from our home in Wash Lane to St Bernard's Monastery, Olton. I remember all the houses we passed in the lane had their curtains drawn, and my mother sobbing through the journey. I remember mother calling out father's name, 'Dennis, Dennis. Oh, my dear Dennis', as his coffin was lowered into the dark earth, and all our relatives surrounding the graveside: aunts, uncles, cousins, gran and grandad, all dressed in sombre black, and for the first time since the news of his death, my tears flowed unabashed.* (Donnelly, *Memories*, p. 5).

During Holy Week, half way between Palm Sunday and Easter, the *Luftwaffe* pounded Birmingham once again. On the night of 9 April 1941, 200 bombers dropped 650 high explosive bombs and 170 sets of incendiaries. As the mayhem began, Irene Edwards dressed her two children in siren suits. The boys were aged eighteen months and four years, and their mom used to put them on the kitchen table, 'my arms around them as we had no shelter'. The house shook from the blasts and Irene's eldest lad looked at her and said, '"Mommy is it because I never ate all my Hot Cross Bun"'. A land mine went off in the next road, his eyes looked so sad. I said, "Of course not darling".' (Letter, 17 July 1996). The first bomb fell on Bordesley Green at 9.35 p.m. Within minutes reports were coming in of high explosive bombs landing in Aston, Small Heath, Stechford and Kings Heath. By early the next morning, much of Birmingham had been battered. Clusters of bombs had struck Saltley, Spring Hill, Ladywood, Holloway Head, Sparkbrook

Fire-fighters in High Street, Birmingham, 10 April 1941.

and Hockley. A trail of explosives followed Summer Lane from Constitution Hill to Gower Street. Another line of explosives had been strung out along Long Acre and Cromwell Street, Nechells. And a mass of bombs and incendiaries had thundered upon Deritend, Highgate and Digbeth.

A 1,000lb bomb exploded on the corner of Steelhouse Lane. The blast killed Inspector Mark Sellek, patrolling the roof of the police station nearby. It blinded temporarily Sergeant Tom Smith and almost severed one of the feet of Chief Inspector John Dodman. Closer to the city centre 'the whole of the Midland Arcade was a mass of flames from High Street to New Street'. The road itself was ablaze and 'a molten stream of blazing tar pushed its way downhill towards New Street Station'. So grave was the situation that senior officers decided to call upon the Royal Engineers to blast a fire break. Before they could do so a large block of buildings collapsed, 'enabling the fire to be cut off without the use of dynamite'. This became known as the Big Top site, until it was redeveloped. As in the previous November, the city's water supply was affected drastically and fire fighters had to draw supplies from bomb craters which had filled with water from the broken mains. (Klopper, *The Fight Against Fire*, p. 91). Birmingham's oldest hotel, the 'Swan' was destroyed, 'The Prince of Wales' in Broad Street was gutted by fire and St Martin's in the Bull Ring was damaged badly. A high explosive bomb fell on the approach way to the western door of the church, making a crater amidst the graves, blowing away pinnacles, and tearing holes in the masonry. In a niche on the western façade, a statue of St Martin was untouched by the blast. ('Bomb Damage in Birmingham', *Birmingham Post*, 17 April 1941).

Ronald Jackson, a probationary constable, witnessed the devastation in Small Heath. He was patrolling the Coventry Road and as the attack intensified, he was sent from one devastated house to another. In some homes he found 'dust covered corpses, one of them sitting on cellar steps in a quiet attitude of resignation, and others with little more than a trickle of blood escaping from the mouth to indicate that their lungs had been burst wide open by the blast'. Later that night Ronald was told to report to the flats in Garrison Lane, Bordesley. A bomb had shattered the floors in one of the blocks, and a concrete block had pinned down a woman who was still alive. The young constable burrowed into the rubble, ignoring the water pouring out from broken pipes and taking care of a precarious wall. He found a crack in the concrete and after receiving a blade with no handle he began to saw at the metal reinforcing rods. It took him an hour to cut the first bar, and then he was able to pull away a square of concrete. This freed the woman's legs, enabling her to be pulled to safety. Ronald Jackson was awarded the George Medal for his valour. (Andrew Moncur, 'Fighting a drunk as the world was being flattened', April 1941. *Evening Mail Special*, April 1981, p.13).

The ferocity of the raid meant that the emergency services were stretched yet again to their utmost. Denis Howell declared that the Fire Brigade and their auxiliary comrades 'fought like Trojans but were totally overwhelmed'. Rescue parties and ambulance personnel 'were working all out but were often unable to get through the rubble to the next incident'. Wardens, firemen and 'the people, whether trained or not, with shrapnel falling all about them, sought to rescue the trapped, put out the fires and comfort the distressed'. (Howell, *Made in Birmingham*, p. 40) In Denis's neighbourhood the 'Lozells' Picture House 'was completely blitzed'. Its manager was Mr Jennings. He was on fire watch duty when the explosives hit the building and killed him. A couple of miles to the east in Nechells, the modern factory of L.H. Newton's was 'reduced in the space of a few hours to a smouldering heap of chaos and rubble'. Suppliers of nuts, bolts, screws, rivets and studs to the Admiralty, the War Office and the Air Ministry, the firm was like many others in Brum - essential to the war effort. For bravery in putting out incendiaries and saving lives, one worker was awarded the George Medal and another the British Empire Medal. (*The Holding Component*. House Magazine of L.H. Newton & Co. Ltd Birmingham, no. 22, March 1952, thanks to Mrs Harvington).

That night Dot Marshall and her family were in the shelter at Newton's. They had fled there because their cellar was flooded. As the bombers came nearer they listened intently: 'the noise was terrifying & I remember my eyes

The wreckage of the 'Prince of Wales' Theatre, Broad Street, 12 May 1941.

were popping and my mom put her hands over my ears - then it happened! The bomb found its target. All hell broke loose - I thought the end of the world had come.' People were yelling and dashing in all directions whilst 'bricks, wood, dust were all falling on us'. Her dad and the other firewatchers had been shot at with machine-gun fire 'but miraculously they were safe' and rescued the folk in the shelter. Dot's sister, Marg, 'stood in frozen shock as a man had his leg blown off' and then they heard 'a woman screaming "my

The blitzed factory of L. H. Newton's, Nechells, 10 April 1941.

baby, my baby"'. She had dropped the child 'in the rush to get out'. Dot's dad rushed back into the shelter to find the baby, while his wife cried out, 'Fred, Fred come back'. At last her husband returned, clutching the baby. The all clear sounded but as they made their way home the sirens wailed once more. With nowhere to shelter 'Dad was racing round like a man gone barmy'. Then word came they had to go to Johnny Wright's factory in Thimblemill Lane, where they were given old blankets. At last the bombing did end:

> and we made our way home. As we turned into High Park Street . . . Mom screamed 'Oh my God, where's the houses?' Yes! Our house had been bombed. All gone - everything! Devastated we went to my Gran's in Walter Street - the doors and windows were blasted out and my Aunt Doll's house was damaged too! Somehow we got through the night - we all pulled together and although we 'roughed it' we were safe. Mom said 'Right let's get going.' Where were we going? We had to traipse the streets looking for an empty house. We found one in Long Acre (No. 30). Mom and Dad did some running around and sorted things out. We moved in, but only after we had cleaned the house out. It was full of rubble and loads of rubbish.
> (Letter, 20 November 1995).

A number of major buildings were hit elsewhere. They included St Chad's Catholic Cathedral and the Queen Elizabeth Hospital, where incendiaries dropped on dry grass. One of the patients was Mr Biffen, the hospital's instrument curator. Although he was 'in considerable pain and discomfort' he dragged a hose from the corridor hydrant to the window, and sprayed the fire bombs with water from the balcony of the third-floor ward . ('Last Blitz', *Birmingham Mail*, 28 August 1942). In the city centre, damage to the General Hospital was more severe and casualties were sent to Lewis's basement. C.J. Rice described the traumatic scene. Glancing at the wide stairway:

it was crammed from side to side with blood-soaked clothing. I went to a place where I could look down on the basement and there lay the unfortunate people of Birmingham, row on row, the air raid victims . . . only the faces of the people lying there were showing. All the faces bore the same reddy-brown colour, caused by brick dust from demolished buildings. Nearly all were badly injured. Here and there a doctor or a nurse was bending over a maimed body but medical attention was minimal. I thought of the wrecked houses, and families anxious to distraction as to the whereabouts of so many victims. Many of them were children. I found the eyes of one face, that of a boy, looking towards me. I went over and spoke to him. He asked faintly where he was. I told him and said I would come back and see him later. When I went back he had died. Many died that Good Friday. (C.J. Rice, 'After A Raid', Imperial War Museum, cited in Ballard, ed, *A City at War*, p. 29).

The morning after the raid reporters went to Victoria Road, Aston. From its junction with Lichfield Road it looked 'as if a tornado had swept it, so heavy was the damage to small property by high explosive bombs'. ('Last Blitz', *Birmingham Mail*, 28 August 1942). Kathleen Dayus had been told that her mom and sister had been killed, and she witnessed similar sights on her way to Camden Drive, Hockley. She stepped 'past slimy, stinking mud, animal bodies and small fires from burning rubber, metal and rags, past buildings blown from their foundations, and men and women trying to salvage some of their treasured belongings'. At last she reached the top of the hill and neighbours from the district 'confirmed the bad news: but I still couldn't believe it until I got half-way down the hill, and saw my brothers Jack, Charlie and Frank, and my sister Liza standing against the school wall weeping with many of Mother's neighbours.' On the floor there were several bodies covered in sacks. As Kathleen tried to look 'which ones were my mother and sister, the wardens quickly pushed me away and told me not any of them bodies were fit to be seen'. (Kathleen Dayus, *All My Days*, London, 1988, p.86).

The only photograph of all the Eastlakes of Bordesley: Leslie (aged 10); John (33, killed whilst fire-watching 17 May 1941; June (8); Ellen (31); Brenda (6); and Barbara (4).

Thankfully, the Germans did not follow up this devastating attack with another of equal fury. The next night they returned in lesser numbers, and there were no further raids until 17 May, when John Eastlake was killed. Aged 33, he and his wife lived at 33, Artillery Street, Bordesley and they had four children - Leslie, June, Brenda and Barbara. The oldest was aged ten, the youngest was four. A land mine fell on the house next door. A baby of the Anderson family died along with John Eastlake, who was fire-watching.

His wife and children were safe in the communal shelter in Garrison Lane Park. Two months beforehand, the family had gone to Jerome's for a photograph to be taken of all of them. It was the only one they ever had. (Letter, June Eastlake, 25 April 1995).

There were sporadic raids on Birmingham until early July 1941, after which the assaults stopped. By now the *Luftwaffe* was pounding the Soviet Union, which had been attacked by Germany on 22 June 1941. Just over five months later Japanese fighter planes attacked the American fleet at Pearl Harbor whilst Japanese troops invaded Malaya and the Philippines. Within a few days Germany and Italy had declared war on the U.S.A. No longer was the Second World War primarily a European conflict; now it was a world war. Faced with a dire battle of attrition to the east, the *Luftwaffe* fitfully resumed its raids on Britain in the summer of 1942. On the morning of 27 July bombs were dropped on the Rover in Solihull, and that evening Birmingham was raided by at least 60 planes. About 283 fires were reported across the city, and phosphorus bombs were dropped close to the Lancaster Street Headquarters of the Fire Brigade. Not far away, in A.B. Row, Duddeston a high explosive fell on the works of Gabriel and Company. During peacetime the firm made stainless steel castings, but it had moved over to making gun mountings, tank track links and electrical fittings for the Royal Navy. The bomb destroyed the offices and part of the works, but within a fortnight production had resumed behind a temporary wooden facade. ('Heavy Attack on Birmingham', *Birmingham Post*, 29 July 1942; Gabriel and Company Ltd. *1884-1984. Centenary*, Birmingham, 1984, p. 11-12).

Unsung Heroine

One night when the sirens were a little late, the bombs had begun to fall.
My mother showed her courage that night, the night she saved us all.
We were caught in the open, when suddenly a blinding flash.
A rush of wind blew over us, then came a deafening crash.

Mom hurled herself upon us then, covering us where we lay.
A piece of debris meant for us, but mom got in the way.
A piece of debris meant for us, a lump of the kitchen door.
She carried the scar upon her back for fifty years or more.

Like so many other mothers her courage did abound.
She protected us with her body as we lay upon the ground.
For years that wound did trouble her, her face would cloud with pain.
But she never mentioned the debt I owed, nor once did she complain.

Such unstinting devotion to duty from they who also served.
Never got the recognition that they so well deserved.
Countless acts of selfless courage, valorous acts unheard.
My mother acted like so many others, an unsung heroine.

Bob Wilkes

This poem describes events on the night of 28 July 1942, when a high explosive bomb hit a water tank in Pavillion Avenue, Smethwick.

As a member of the Home Guard, Mr Dutton was patrolling the railway line by Soho Road. The night was 'brilliantly clear' and the noise of German bombers was obvious. Yet there were no sirens. Then 'with a terrible, shocking suddenness there were several huge explosions close by'. His girlfriend, Midge Maiden, lived with her family in Rookery Road - which was in the direction of the blasts. Midge and her sister and brother were sent by their mother to the shelter in the garden. Just as they entered it 'we heard the terrible scream of a bomb and a dreadful noise'. The teenagers were trapped until a neighbour dug them out. When they emerged into the moonlight they had an incredible shock. Nothing was left of their home and both sides of the road were flattened. Their mother and older sister 'had paused to collect blankets for us and were killed, but it was a fortnight before it was confirmed to us'. A widow, Elsie Maiden's 'last thoughts and actions were to serve us'. (Letter, 10 May 1995). Norah Jones, then Davis, lived in the same road. Her neighbours, 'the Priestmans, Bonds and eleven other poor souls died that night'. When her dad, Albert, came out of the Anderson Shelter 'all he could see was the Purus clock way across the road - no houses left just a scatter of rubble, and his first remark was, "Well, Our Glad (Mom) will be pleased, we've got rid of the mice at last." A true Brit!' (Letter, April, 1996).

Summer Hill was devastated in the same way as was Rookery Road. In the blasted areas a number of people had lucky escapes. Rupert Cash was on the roof of the church at which he was caretaker. He had a stirrup pump hose and was prepared to

The ruins of Rookery Road, Handsworth, 28 July 1942.

put out any incendiaries before the timber roofing could be set alight. The building next door was hit. Rupert was blown off his feet but managed to keep hold of his hose. It felt loose, and when he looked at it he saw that 'it had been cut in two by some flying missile, which must have passed me no more than six inches away'. As he made his way downstairs 'there was a tremendous crash of falling masonry', and he was fortunate not to be buried. Elsewhere in the city a bomb had wrecked the house of an elderly Welsh woman from Aberystwyth. She had sheltered under the stairs and the door of a cupboard fell on her, wounding her head. A reporter asked her whether now she would go back to her 'Welsh mountains'. Her answer was firm: 'No, I think I'll stick it out now, I've made some good friends in this town'. ('Eight Down', *Birmingham Mail*, 28 July 1942).

The last main raid on Birmingham took place on 30 July when incendiaries 'came down in showers' and 'there were grievous happenings in poorer quarters where houses hit by the explosive bombs collapsed on the inmates'. Amongst the dead were a mother and her four children. ('Fire Raiders Foiled', *Birmingham Post*, 31 July 1942). There were no more attacks until 23 April 1943 when the Germans assault on Brum ended as it began. A lone pilot dropped bombs over Drummond Rd, Little Bromwich, injuring eighteen people. By this date the prospects of victory for the Allies had increased. The British had defeated Rommel and his North Afrika Korps, the Soviets had forced

The VJ Day party in Holland Road, Aston, 15 August 1945.

the German 6th Army to surrender at Stalingrad, and the United States of America had halted Japanese expansion in the Pacific at the Battle of Midway. In September 1943, Italy surrendered and early in the new year a massive Soviet offensive flung the German forces back to the west. Then, on 6 June 1944, known as D-Day, British, American and Canadian troops made successful landings in Normandy. The Germans put up stiff resistance and not until 2 May 1945 did Berlin fall to the Red Army. Within days German forces had capitulated everywhere.

On 8 May Victory in Europe day was welcomed with celebrations throughout the United Kingdom. There were tens of thousands of street parties. The one in Millward Street, Small Heath was organised by Arthur Blinko. He had been discharged from the army in 1943, and once D-Day had taken place he began making plans for a big knees-up at the end of the war. He went to Guy's Brewery in Vauxhall and asked to have put by 'so many bottles of beer and pop'. He left a deposit for his order and told the manager he was not sure when he would need it, but that when 'Peace Day' came 'I don't want Millward Street to run short'. Each Sunday his daughter, Enid, collected 6d 'from each house, and whatever the lady of the house could spare - a couple of spoonfuls of sugar, a spoonful of tea, a packet of custard, a jelly and of course food coupons'. Arthur himself would 'tour the food warehouses and with his wonderful smile and happy disposition he would come home with large tins of fruit and sometimes butter'. When V.E. Day was announced, Millward Street was ready. It was a 'great day, fancy dress and tea party and every child had a bible and later the pianos came out and we danced until dawn'. (Letter, 8 May 1995). There were more festivities on14 August when Victory against Japan Day was proclaimed. At last, the United Kingdom was at peace.

The Effect of the Raids on Birmingham

Between 25 June 1940 and 15 May 1944 Birmingham had received 2,061 air raid messages of all kinds. Of these, 365 were 'Red' warnings and the sirens had sounded. Seventy-seven of these alerts were followed by raids. Some of them ran into each other, giving a figure of 65 separate attacks. The *Luftwaffe* dropped 5,129 high explosive bombs, including 930 which did not go off; 48 parachute mines, of which sixteen did not explode; scores of thousands of incendiaries; and a number of oil and phosphorus bombs. In all about 2,000 tons of bombs were dropped on Birmingham and 4,863 fires were reported. The raids destroyed 12,391 houses, and damaged tens of thousands more; they wrecked 302 factories, and affected badly hundreds of others; they obliterated 34 churches, halls and cinemas, and harmed hundreds more; and they blew up 205 other buildings. But the greatest loss of all was the loss of life. German air raids killed 2,241 Brummies, including 211 children under sixteen; they injured seriously 3,010 people and slightly wounded another 3,682. (Black, *History of the Corporation*, pp. 87-8).

In 1944 an editorial in the *Birmingham Post* stated that bomb 'damage was never immediately obvious to strangers and had to be looked for'. This was written three years after the worst raids - after much debris had been removed, most bomb sites had been cleared, and a great proportion of damaged property had been repaired. Observers would have had a different view if they had visited Birmingham in the winter of 1940 and the spring of 1941. Whole roads had been laid waste, great factories had been blasted, churches and shops had been obliterated, craters abounded and destruction was obvious in numerous districts. On 5 December 1940 Holly Cartwright, deputy civil defence chief of Birmingham, actually did arrange a tour of the city for senior military figures and Government officials. From Paradise Street they turned left into Suffolk Street where they saw the gutted store of a railway company and demolished premises at the back of Warwick Hire Company's Garage. Nearby, Holloway Head was a scene of havoc whilst there was extensive damage on both sides of Smallbrook Street. Turning left into Bromsgrove Street the visitors were shown the tragic rubble of Kent Street Baths. Moving on to Bradford Street they noticed the damaged Meat Market, whilst in Rea Street they were struck by the number of works of Fisher and Ludlow which had been hit by bombs. From here they went across Bordesley High Street and down the Coventry Road, stopping at an A.R.P. station which had been hit twice by high explosive bombs. Making its way into Small Heath, 'which has repeatedly been the target of enemy attack', the party ended its tour at the B.S.A. ('Tourist trip around the sites', *April 1941. Evening Mail Special*, April 1981, p. 7).

Despite widespread devastation, the Germans failed in disrupting industry seriously. On 5 September 1940, an American reporter felt that the 'output for the whole of the Birmingham area has not been cut more than 5 per cent'. ('Raid Survey', *Birmingham Mail*, 5 September 1940). It is likely that this figure was higher in the immediate aftermath of the terrible raids of November 1940. The important munitions firm of Fisher and Ludlow's lost 40% of its 1,000,0000 square feet of floor space, whilst production at the B.S.A. was affected so adversely that Churchill himself was alarmed. In January 1941 he sent a memorandum to the Minister of Supply. This indicated that the number of rifles manufactured nationally had plummeted from 9,586 in August 1940 to 4,743 by

December. Churchill understood 'that this fall is due to raids on Small Heath, Birmingham'. (Churchill, *The Second World War. Volume III*, p. 644) By March 1941 the B.S.A. had increased its output substantially, thanks to repairs at Armoury Road, the endeavours of managers and workers, and the dispersal of production.

According to Angus Calder, 'though frequently visited', Birmingham 'was let off lightly for its size and importance'. (Angus Calder, *The People's War. Britain 1939-45*, London, 1971 edn, p.254). Similarly, Sutcliffe and Smith stress that Birmingham was bombed more heavily than most British places but that the city's ordeal 'was relatively insignificant when compared to that endured by most German cities'. (Sutcliffe and Smith, *Birmingham 1939-70*, pp. 31-3). No-one should disregard the terrible effects of bombing wherever it occurred. Anyone with compassion

The Bull Ring after the raid of 9 April 1941. The buildings by Moor Street are in ruins, but the steeple of St Martin's rises up amidst the destruction.

must sympathise with the anguish of innocent people whoever they were and whatever their nationality. Many Germans were not Nazis and some of them were victims of the megalomania of Hitler. And many of them suffered in British air raids. But in recognising the misery, distress and perseverance of others, there is a tendency amongst some writers to diminish the torment, pain and firmness of the British people. Thousands of them were killed, tens of thousands were hurt, scores of thousands lost all their possessions, and countless thousands had their hopes dashed, their expectations ruined and their emotions scraged. For all the woes inflicted upon them their morale did not collapse, their purpose did not waver and their patriotism did not wane. Each morning after an air raid they comforted each other, they helped each other, they cleared up the mess, and they went to work.

In particular, Birmingham was not let off lightly. Only in Liverpool and London were more people killed in the Blitz than in Brum, and only the capital was more heavily bombed. Another factor should be borne in mind. Although bombs did fall across the whole of Birmingham, the bulk of explosives landed in a more confined part of the city. In effect this was the main evacuation zone, excluding the district around Bournbrook. This area of main bombing ran from the boundary with West Bromwich at Handsworth and went down Holyhead Road, up Albert Road and Holly Road and along Hamstead Road and Wellington Road. It crossed the Birchfield Road, followed Aston Lane, went up Deykin Avenue, Witton, came down past Salford Reservoir and crossed the Tyburn Road into Aston Church Road. From there it stretched across the southern edges of Ward End Park and then struck south along Naseby Road and Anthony Road, Alum Rock. Continuing in a south-easterly direction it trailed Churchill Road in Bordesley Green, Blake Lane in Little Bromwich, and Hob Moor Road. Thence it switched to the course of the River Cole and moved south west along the eastern boundaries of Small Heath and Greet. From there it split Sparkhill, going down Avondale Road and along Court Road and Woodstock Road. It entered Balsall Heath at Newport Road and went on to Edgbaston Road, after which it turned north with the flow of the River Rea. At Belgrave Road it went west up Lee Bank, across Five Ways and along the Hagley Road until it struck along Portland Road. The line then stuck to the boundaries with Smethwick and finally West Bromwich.

At its greatest extent this area was not more than four and a quarter miles in length and five and a half miles in width. Often the distances were less, but if the largest possible space is calculated then it included 14,960 acres. Birmingham as a whole was 51,147 acres. Consequently the large majority of bombs fell in less than a third of the city's land. This assessment has important implications. Officially one high explosive bomb was dropped for every ten acres in the city. The ratio would be much lower if the number of bombs per acre was calculated for the main evacuation area. Similarly, the proportion of people who died was much higher in this zone.

No-one should diminish the sturdiness of those who survived the Blitz, wherever they lived and worked. Every night from 7 September until the end of November, Londoners endured severe raids. In those three months alone, 36,000 explosives struck the capital and 12,696 people died. Proportionately more people were killed in Hull than anywhere else, whilst Yarmouth endured more raids than either Liverpool or Birmingham. Blitzed towns and cities should not be put in a macabre league table based on the numbers of deaths and the tonnage of bombs dropped. The people of Birmingham do not wish to detract from the bravery of citizens elsewhere. They do not seek special attention. But for 56 years the effects of the Blitz on Birmingham have been censored, minimised or ignored. Brummies ask only for the same treatment as other cities. They wish for recognition.

BIRMINGHAM EVACUATION AREA

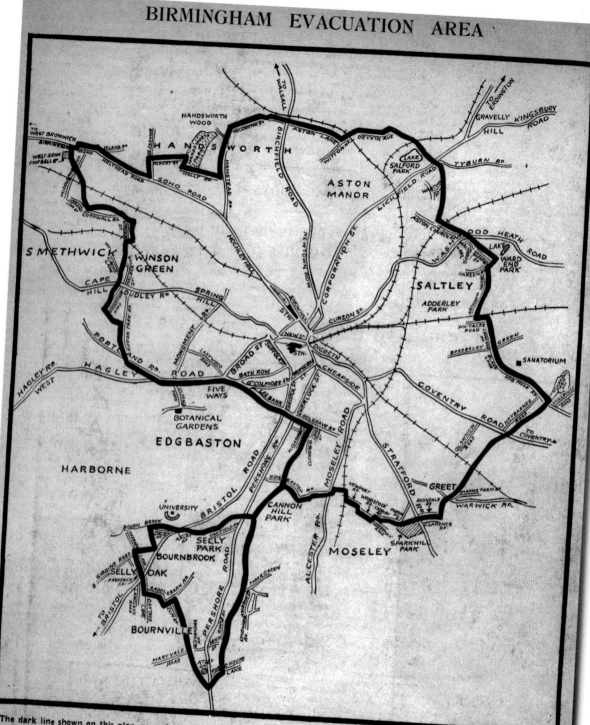

The dark line shown on this plan, as enclosing the central part of Birmingham with the additional triangular patch in the Selly Park area, marks the area from which children are to be evacuated. In fact the area does not end at the Smethwick boundary, but will be continued so as to enclose the densely populated parts of that town.

VE Day Remembered

What did you do on VE Day dad?

I can't really remember son, I was only a lad.

We had a street party, a bonfire and fireworks too.

The old folks made it quite a to do.

There was bunting strung across the street

And we sang and danced at Hitler's defeat.

The men had a barrel from the 'Pump Tavern' pub

And despite the rationing we had loads of grub.

Our victory songs rang out in snatches,

And we marvelled at the colours of the Bengal matches.

Billy Pursall acted the clown,

Running up a ladder and sliding down.

Old Granny Crompton sat out all day,

Smoking baccy in a pipe made of clay.

The fireworks were a treat that night.

All coloured and smoky and really bright.

When the fire died down it was quite late,

Staying up was really a treat.

I went up to bed smelling of smoke and dirt,

And as a real treat I slept in my shirt.

There you are son, as you heard me say,

I can't really remember Victory in Europe Day.

Arthur Wilkes

AFTERWORD

This book has been about how Brummies contributed to victory in the Second World War in Birmingham. It has not been about the tens of thousands of Brummies who were involved in the conflict elsewhere. Their contribution to the battle against tyranny cannot be ignored. They included Agnes Dameau of Namur, Belgium. Formerly Agnes Thompson of Birmingham, she was imprisoned by the Gestapo for hiding an escaped British prisoner. Such steadfastness was as obvious amongst the Brummie men who served in the forces and the Merchant Navy. Amongst their number were Flight Lieutenant Ian Scott who led the first air raid on Germany in 1939, and Stanley Streeter, a navigator who was killed on 2 April 1943. After his death his parents commissioned a painting of him as St George and hung it in St Jude's Church, Hill Street. Airmen such as these were supported by the bravery of ground crew like leading aircraftman Joseph White, a nursing orderly. In April 1943 he and a colleague saved a gunner from the blazing wreckage of a Wellington bomber. Joseph was awarded the British Empire Medal. ('Birmingham Heroine Who Defied the Gestapo', *Sunday Mercury*, 10 September 1944; 'Kings Norton Old Boy Leads First Raid', *Sutton Coldfield News*, 23 September 1939; Patricia Chapman, Letter, 14 August 1995; *London Gazette*, 23 July 1943, thanks to Steve White).

RAF ground crew celebrating the end of the war in a tent in Germany. Early in the morning of 7 May 1945 their squadron leader woke them, told them the news and gave them a bottle of whisky. Lying at the front is John Bell, a Geordie who came to Brum in the Depression and married Kitty Warwick of Studley Street, Sparkbrook. Before he was called up in 1941 he worked at the BSA. On 22 November 1940, he almost lost his right foot when a fire bomb exploded by his leg when he was fire-watching in the yard of the 'Gate'.

The Royal Air Force won the Battle of Britain. As important a victory was the long-drawn out Battle of the Atlantic, when merchant seamen and sailors of the Royal Navy defied German U-boats to bring much-needed supplies to the United Kingdom. Many of these men were killed and others were dreadfully mutilated. A similar fate befell thousands of soldiers, amongst them Stan Smith of the Dorset Regiment. In the assault on Hill 121 after D-Day he was blasted by a mortar bomb and immediately knew he had lost his left eye. He was flown back to England and had 49 operations to rebuild his face. (Letter, 1995, thanks to Dora Hill). Other men spent terrible years in captivity, such as did Dennis Timmington. He was in Singapore when it was surrendered to the Japanese on 15 February 1941. Much of his imprisonment was spent at the infamous Changi camp and then at the notorious Tarso camp where he was forced to labour on the 'Railway of Death'. (Stan Smith, Letter, 1995, thanks to Dora Hill; 'Seamen are the Forgotten Heroes', Dennis Etchells, R.W. Ellis and S. Davis, Letters to the *Evening Mail*, 8 May 1995; Dennis Timmington, Letter, August 1995, thanks to Doris Armstrong).

Often airmen, soldiers, sailors and merchant seamen returned home after a long absence. Mrs P. Morris's dad was in the Royal Electrical and Mechanical Engineers Corps and had been sent to North Africa in February 1941, 'leaving my mother 4 months pregnant and with 3 other children to look after'. His wife received a message that he would come back to Birmingham about 24 June and 'being the wonderful mom she was she managed to get us all new clothes in which to meet him'.

The destruction of St Thomas's, Bath Row, bombed on 11 December 1940. Many of the church's treasures were saved by a member of the congregation, Ernest Mason. Fittingly the ruins are now part of the Peace Gardens.

By dinner-time there was no news of the train that we were waiting for so we were advised to go and get something to eat. So Mom took us home for a quick snack - then back again to wait. Later that day a kindly porter told us that the train we were waiting for would not be in until possibly early the next morning so we were better off at home. So very reluctantly we went home once more. I remember sitting on the front step until about 10 p.m. - then we all went to lie on our beds fully dressed. The next thing I remember was hearing mom, my elder sister and brother rushing down stairs - I followed as fast as I could. There in the hallway was a very deeply tanned man - my dad. It was such a wonderful feeling. When he went away I was 4½ years old, now here was the baby he left nearly 9 yrs old. Nothing can replace how we all felt that time - even now it makes me feel so full of warmth and love. (Letter, 22 February 1995).

Not everyone came home. Millions of people died in Europe, Asia, and Africa. They lost their lives because some men and women were consumed by hatred for those who were different to them. The need to stand up to intolerance and prejudice is made plain throughout the world by the countless thousands of cemeteries in which lie those who died in the Second World War. Those Brummies who were killed in the blitz are recalled in a memorial at the Peace Gardens in Bath Row. It is an appropriate setting. The gardens include the west bell tower of St Thomas's Church, all that is left of the building after it was bombed at 7.25 p.m. on 11 December 1940. Destroyed by violence, the remnants of the church are a poignant symbol of peace and reconciliation. On the entrance below the bell tower there is a plaque. It states: 'In memory of those citizens of Birmingham who died or were injured as a result of the extensive air raids on this city between August 1940 and April 1943'. The memorial was unveiled in 1995 on the 50th anniversary of V.E. Day. We shall remember.

When the Lights Went On

I stood with Our Mom on the top of the hill,
We watched as the lights all came on.
It was the end of the war, the blackout too,
At last the darkness had gone.
As a child I remember the blackouts well,
I remember growing up in the dark.
We had to be ever so careful,
We couldn't even show a spark.
You see, if we did, Gerry would know,
He would know where to drop them bombs,
And make no mistake he'd move real fast,
He'd drop em, and blow up our homes.
What a beautiful sight, just look at them lights
Twinkling all over the place.
How pretty they look, I looked up at Mom,
She was wiping a tear from her face.
'Thank God', she said, 'Thank God it's over.'
She held my hand tight.
We ran down the hill as fast as we could
Into those magical lights.

Pat Hambidge, 'A Brummie Wench'

BOOK LIST

Birmingham Central Library, Chamberlain Square is the place to go if you want to do further research on war-time Brum. On the sixth and seventh floors, Local Studies and History and Archives have war-time photographs, copies of all the Birmingham newspapers, and much other primary evidence relating to the war.

The following are general books recommended for people wanting to begin research. Specific studies can be found in the text.

John V. Abbott, *Raiders Past. Air Raids on Yardley,* Studley, Brewin, 1993 ISBN 1858580196

Phillada Ballard, ed, *A City at War. Birmingham 1939-1945*, Birmingham, Birmingham Museum and Art Gallery, 1985 ISBN 0709301308

Birmingham City Council, *Waiting for the All Clear. Life in Birmingham during the Second World War*, Birmingham, 1995 ISBN 0709302096

H. J. Black, *History of the Corporation of Birmingham. Volume VI. 1936-1950*, Birmingham, General Purposes Committee for the Corporation of Birmingham,1957

Angus Calder, *The People's War. Britain 1939-45*, London, Cape, 1992 ISBN 19710712652841

Kathleen Dayus, *All My Days*, London, Virago,1988 ISBN 0860680762

J.A.S. Grenville, *The Collins History of the World in the Twentieth Century*, London, Harper Collins,1994 ISBN 0002551691

Tom Harrisson, *Living Through the Blitz*, London, Collins,1976 ISBN 0002160099

Denis Howell, *Made in Birmingham. The Memoirs of Denis Howell*, London, Queen Anne (Macdonald),1990 ISBN 0356176452

Zoë Josephs, *Survivors. Jewish Refugees in Birmingham* 1933-1945, Oldbury, Meridian,1988 ISBN 1869922026

Richard Shackleton, *The Second World War*, London, Historical Association, 1991 ISBN 0852783299

Anthony Sutcliffe and Roger Smith, History of Birmingham. Volume III. Birmingham 1939-1970, London, 1974 ISBN 0192151827

A.J.P. Taylor, *The Second World War. An illustrated history*, London, Hamilton1975 ISBN 0241892058

Edwin Webb and John Duncan, *Blitz Over Britain*, Speldhurst, Kent, Spellmount, 1990 ISBN 0946771898

SUBJECT INDEX